POWER
AND
WEALTH

THE POLITICAL ECONOMY
OF INTERNATIONAL RELATIONS
SERIES
Edited by Benjamin J. Cohen

POWER AND WEALTH:
The Political Economy of International Power
by Klaus Knorr

FORTHCOMING *

THE CHARITY OF NATIONS:
The Political Economy of Aid
by David Wall

THE POLITICAL ECONOMY OF IMPERIALISM
by Benjamin J. Cohen

THE POLITICAL ECONOMY OF
ECONOMIC GROWTH AND INTERNATIONAL CHANGE
by Robert G. Gilpin

THE POLITICAL ECONOMY OF INTERNATIONAL TRADE
by William H. Branson

THE POLITICAL ECONOMY OF INTERNATIONAL MONEY
by Raymond F. Mikesell

THE POLITICAL ECONOMY OF
INTERNATIONAL COMMUNIST RELATIONS
by Franklyn D. Holzman

* All book titles are tentative.

POWER AND WEALTH

THE POLITICAL ECONOMY OF INTERNATIONAL POWER

KLAUS KNORR

BASIC BOOKS, INC., PUBLISHERS

NEW YORK

© 1973 by Basic Books, Inc.

Library of Congress Catalog Card Number: 72–89187

SBN 465–06140–0

Manufactured in the United States of America

DESIGNED BY VINCENT TORRE

73 74 75 76 77 10 9 8 7 6 5 4 3 2 1

EDITOR'S PREFACE

Benjamin J. Cohen

Students of international relations have long been aware of the interconnections between the politics and the economics of their subject. Classical and medieval writers always emphasized the dynamic interaction of the two factors in relations between states and between nations. Likewise, mercantilist writers repeatedly emphasized the reciprocity that existed between economic policy and national power. Even Adam Smith, the great foe of the mercantilists, admitted the relevance of political considerations in discussing issues of public economy. It was Smith who allowed that despite the attractions of free trade, tariffs might be advisable on grounds of national security. "Defense," he said, "is of much more importance than opulence."

It was only in the nineteenth century, with the gradual development of the two separate disciplines of economics and political science, that the interconnections between economics and politics in international relations came to be de-emphasized. Economics evolved as the study of welfare and of issues relating to the allocation of scarce resources, political science as the study of power and of issues relating to the resolution of conflicting interests. Gradually most economists and political scientists (other than Marxist theorists) began to act as if "never the twain shall meet." And as a result, they rarely do. The bulk of the modern, conventional literature on international relations is curiously dichotomous. International economists write about international economics, political scientists write about international politics—and a gulf exists between them which, if anything, seems to grow wider and deeper with every passing year. Only rarely does one find an economist rash enough to address himself analytically to the political dimensions of international economic problems or a political scientist headstrong enough to apply economic theory to the analysis of international power relations. These few exceptions simply cannot suffice to bridge the gap. For the most part, the two disciplines conduct what amounts to a dialogue of the deaf.

That the gap ought to be bridged should of course be obvious. This is an era of rapidly increasing interdependence in international economic relations. It is also an era of rapidly increasing state intervention in economic affairs. Nations, now more than ever, have a need to understand both the politics and the economics of their subject, to combine and integrate both of these factors within a single analytical framework—in short, to develop a proper *political economy* of international relations.

This series is designed to help students of international relations in moving toward that objective. The initial stimulus for the series was the publication of Charles Kindleberger's admirable pioneering work, *Power and Money* (Basic Books, 1970). Here at last was a book explicitly intended to fill the gap between international economics and international politics. However, as Kindleberger himself admitted, no single volume could possibly pretend to develop a comprehensive political economy of international relations entirely on its own. His volume sufficed mainly to define the problem and to suggest some of its over-all dimensions. The seven volumes in the present series are intended to build outward from his work, to further explore various aspects of the problem at greater length and in considerably greater detail. Each will be designed to provide supplementary reading in courses on international economics or international politics. Each will be devoted to a single topic under the broad heading of international relations.

It is appropriate that the first volume in the series to appear is Klaus Knorr's. For what could be more central to the political economy of international relations than power? Power is at the heart of the relations between nations, and economics and politics are at the heart of the concept of national power. Yet few topics in international relations are so poorly understood. In the literature in this area there is remarkably little consensus about, for example, what determines national power in the international arena, or how power can be utilized, or what its consequences may be. In fact, most writers do not even seem to be sure what power *is*.

Professor Knorr addresses himself to these and related issues. His procedure is, first, to systematically delineate the dimensions of the concept of power, and then to carefully explore its separate bases and uses. At each stage of the analysis, economics and politics are skillfully woven into a common intellectual fabric. Much of the discussion is (necessarily) conducted at a rather abstract level of conceptualization. But much also is devoted to practical evaluation of a quite wide range of historical experience. A number of interesting conclusions come out of this study which are summarized in the final chapter. One suspects that these are bound to stimulate considerable thought and research in this vital area of scholarship.

PREFACE

It is important to read this preface in order to appreciate the nature and limitations of this book. When first asked to write it for the series of which it is part, I assented because I was more intrigued by the idea than held back by the apparent difficulties of the task. Even at that stage, the difficulties seemed daunting. "Power and Wealth" is so obvious a title for a book one would want to read that it would have been written, and written more than once, if it could be done. The difficulty, of course, lies in the requirements that the author possess the skills of at least two disciplines (economics and political science) and preferably more (e.g. history); the ability to search and use the findings of several disparate literatures; the audacity to improvise about problems which have not attracted much research; and to weld the various components into an intelligible and useful synthesis. Nevertheless, I decided it was worth trying, even if the result was bound to be uneven.

After two years of work, I know that the difficulties are even greater than I assumed at the outset. Yet I do not regret having made the commitment. It is clear that only a collective effort would assure a sufficient range of expertise. But it is unlikely that collaboration by authors from different disciplines would produce sufficient intellectual integration. This can probably be achieved only by a single author, even if at the cost of unevenness of product and a degree of idiosyncrasy.

Another difficulty arose from the request to write a small volume of approximately 60,000 words. This turned out to be very stultifying, especially in view of the prevailing ambiguity about the very conceptualization of power and influence, even in the best academic literature. This made it necessary to present such a conceptual scheme in considerable detail. Soon I found myself planning and writing a large book, and to write and publish a large volume is what I intend to do. In trying to discharge my obligation to do a small book first, I encountered a difficult job of compression and selection. While I have a growing collection of case studies concerning uses of power, most empirical material had to be sacrificed. So did entire subjects to which separate chapters will be devoted in the larger study, especially a systematic analysis of noncoercive influence, informal penetration, international interdependence, and imperialism and neocolonialism. I hope, nevertheless, that the present book—fragmentary though it is—will prove worthwhile, and reactions to it should help me in performing the larger task. In a way, the high conceptual context of the present study is a virtue. The conceptual framework invites readers to integrate what they have learned about the real world in bits and pieces.

Some colleagues and students have read and usefully commented on various drafts. Professor Benjamin J. Cohen of the Fletcher School of Law and Diplomacy gave valuable advice, especially on selecting the present volume from a much larger manuscript. I want to thank particularly the Center of International Studies for providing much appreciated secretarial and similar assistance.

KLAUS KNORR

Princeton, 1972

CONTENTS

POWER
AND
WEALTH

CHAPTER

1

Power and Influence

Since interstate relations involve the distribution, creation, and destruction of such common values as security and wealth, governments are often eager to exercise power and influence and are, in turn, subject to the power and influence of other governments. The academic literature on "power" and "influence" is in a deplorable state of confusion and disagreement. Yet the usefulness of these terms is measured by a clear conception of what power and influence mean, of the conditions under which they will be wielded, and of the consequences of their employment. To promote such clarity is the purpose of this chapter.

Coercion, Noncoercive Influence, and Noncoercive Uses of Power

Power can be used either to establish influence by means of coercion or, without coercive intent to defend or change the status quo between actors. An actor (B) is influenced if he adapts his behavior in compliance with, or in anticipation of, another actor's (A) demands, wishes, or proposals. B's conduct is then affected by something A does or by something he expects A may do. In consequence, *B* will modify his behavior if he would not have done so otherwise, or he will not change his behavior if he would have altered it in the absence of external influence.

Influence can be noncoercive as well as coercive. It is *coercive* when *B*'s conduct is affected by his fear of sanctions of one kind or another: that is, some threat, actual or imputed, to his goal achievement. *B*'s choice of behavior is consequently restricted by *A*'s influence. On the other hand, influence is *noncoercive,* if *B*'s choices are enriched rather than limited by *A*'s influence, for example—if *A* persuades *B* that a proposed co-operative venture is mutually beneficial. In the event of coercion, *B* loses, or expects to lose, something of value while *A* gains, or expects to gain, something of value. When influence is noncoercive, both *A* and *B* gain, or expect to gain, something valuable. Some writers use the term "power" to designate all influence, whether coercive or noncoercive. In this study, we will designate only coercive influence as power.

Coercion, however, is not the only purpose for exercising power. It can also be used directly to modify the status quo between actors without an attempt to secure compliance. Coercion is effected by a threat of punishment, for example, the threat of war. Yet, the military capability on which such a threat is based can also be used simply to take something (e.g. a piece of territory) from an opponent or, conversely, to keep an opponent by sheer resistance from taking it. There may be no attempt to coerce the opponent to give up territory or to make him desist from attempting to seize it. In any particular situation of conflict, to be sure, military force may be used for both these purposes at once. But the two purposes are distinct. A noncoercive purpose would be to destroy part of a potential opponent's military capacity. Thus, in 1803, a British fleet sailed into Copenhagen harbor at a time of peace and carried off the Danish navy. Or, after China had been testing nuclear explosives, there was considerable speculation, in 1968 and 1969, whether the Soviet Union might not simply wipe out the Chinese nuclear establishment by bombardment. Reducing a potential opponent's military capability may, of course, set him up for coercion. But this may not be the actual purpose. The object might be simply to render a state too weak to attack others. Similarly, the capacity to withhold economic advantages may be used for other than coercive purposes. Thus, after World War II, the United States placed an embargo on the export of a wide range of "strategic goods" to the Soviet Union. The object then was not to coerce Russia to do something or other, but to obstruct the growth of her military strength. A state may also infiltrate another politically by means of propaganda, bribery, conspiratorial support of revolutionaries, etc. Again, the purpose may be coercive; but it may also be only to weaken politically the other state or its government by fostering domestic disunity.

In domestic law enforcement, the purpose of punishment is either to coerce (i.e. deter) or to curtail the ability of the criminal to pursue crime. In other social relationships, another purpose of punishment is to afford emotional satisfaction. Similarly in interstate relationships, power may be used not only in order to coerce or to affect an actor's capabilities, but also in order simply to hurt another, to inflict vengeance, or to symbolize displeasure or antagonism. For example, Peking's refusal in the 1960's to recognize and exchange diplomatic representation with countries eager to reciprocate did not serve a coercive purpose, and the same can be said about the nonrecognition of China by the United States. Also, by the late 1960's, it had become clear that most goods which the United States government did not permit to be exported to the Soviet Union did not in fact obstruct that country's military development. The effect was that of an economic pinprick which had come to serve a symbolic purpose. (Although this study concerns all uses of power, it will focus mainly on coercive power, partly because this use is less easily understood than the alternative uses just mentioned, but chiefly because the coercive employment of power is more frequent than its noncoercive use.)

The Forms of Power and of Noncoercive Influence

Power and noncoercive influence appear in forms that are specified with reference to the particular base from which influence is
generated. Thus, we have just distinguished between military
power, economic power, and political penetrative power. Military
power turns on threats which can take various particular forms
(e.g. an increase in the military budget, the mobilization of military reserves, redeployment of naval forces, and even war itself
if it expresses a threat to continue or escalate existing hostilities).
Economic power turns on the withholding of economic advantages
(e.g. trade, investment, currency support, development aid). Political penetrative power, which is less well understood, turns on
a variety of overt or clandestine activities (e.g. propaganda, the
fomenting of political unrest and strikes, the support of opposition
parties or revolutionary groups, the bribing of officials or political
leaders). In the late 1930's, Nazi Germany employed such means
in order to soften Austria's and Czechoslovakia's resistance. A
favorite technique of Soviet propagandists has been the establishment of "front organizations" (e.g. the World Federation of Trade
Unions, the World Federation of Democratic Youth, and the
World Peace Movement) in non-Communist countries. Propaganda is the planned dissemination of information, arguments and
appeals designed to influence the beliefs, thoughts and actions of
specific foreign target groups. Control achieved by such intervention can be used for making threats, that is, for attempting coercion. This has rightly been called "psychic coercion." [1] More
often it is employed to limit another state's capacity for international action, for example, by creating disunity in the target
country. Alternatively, it can also be used to enlarge a state's
capacity for international action, for instance, by strengthening
the domestic support of a foreign government.

Noncoercive influence affords interaction which is fruitful and
enriches rather than restricts choices for the actors concerned.
Like power, it turns on a large range of values important to these

actors. In fact, any value which is a power base may also provide a base for noncoercive influence. For instance, while the withholding of diplomatic recognition of states and the rupture of diplomatic relations constitute power plays, the extension of recognition and the assumption of diplomatic relations—while also capable of being used coercively—can also provide a base for influence. Even propaganda can be supportive rather than subversive. The essential difference is that A has something of value to B and gives it to B *without condition,* or without any condition that limits B's choice of behavior. For instance, A may give economic assistance to B in order to enable the latter to increase his capacity for economic production. In this case, wealth is the influence base. Similarly, military power may figure as an influence base when it supplies security for another state; expertise is the base when technical assistance is extended. However, as we shall see below, it is questionable whether noncoercive influence is involved whenever any of these values are extended on the basis of a *quid pro quo.*

The extension of information, persuasion, and advice are important bases of noncoercive influence. B may have misunderstood what A is after, and A supplies information in order to dispel misunderstanding. Thus, some interstate conflicts of interest decrease or vanish, once the governments involved are fully informed. Persuasion and advice are related bases of influence. B may have adequate information but may misinterpret it. By means of persuasion, A may help B to redefine their relationship and to evaluate properly the consequences of either's policy. Advice is to suggest a course of action conducive to B's as well as A's goal achievement. It is quite different from a demand, which is to serve exclusively the ends of the demanding actor. Information, persuasion, and advice clarify or enlarge the recipient's choice of policy. A frequent object of persuasion and advice is to propose some co-operative enterprise (such as an alliance or a cultural exchange program) from which both actors can secure value. The play of noncoercive influence and co-operation are facilitated when the value preferences of actors converge rather than diverge—for instance when they share an interest in freer trade or economic integration, or in some sort of ideological utopia. But a similar structure of value preferences proves integrative rather than divisive only if it is marked by priorities that are susceptible to co-operative solution, rather than conflict and competition. Against this background, benevolent influence also thrives on the mutual respect and esteem of elites and communities—feelings which, in the modern age, are rooted in the domestic as well as international performance of countries and often also in dedication to the same ideology. Still more favorable, of course, are special relationships of friendship and trust established as a result of a satisfactory shared past experience. Such relationships impede the exercise of coercion and encourage noncoercive influence, whereas settled relations of animosity have the opposite effect. Trust refers to expectations of benevolent behavior in contrast to suspicion, which feeds on the expectation of malevolence. Although attitudes of respect and friendship may be unrelated to the immediate issues confronting governments, they create an ambiance facilitating co-operation.

All these factors may play a role when international leadership is not hegemony or domination and hence is not derived from compulsion or from a forcible change or maintenance of the *status quo,* either of which, in turn, may be based on military or economic superiority or superiority in some other value. In international interaction, a state may lead by proposing, initiating, and organizing co-operative arrangements redounding to the benefit of all voluntary participants. Thus, the leader may provide and/ or organize military security against aggression or, more generally, the preservation of the established order. Or the leading nation may prove innovating in designing new solutions to pressing problems, for instance by proposing regional federation or other modifications of the *status quo.* The point is that, in the absence of any compulsion, these capacities for organizing co-operation and multinational problem-solving and for increasing the supply of protection and other values furnish the bases for benevolent leadership. This leader does not command, control, and manipulate. He serves his function by information, persuasion, advice, and example. And once a state has displayed these qualities over some time, it enjoys a corresponding prestige that tends to facilitate the future exercise of noncoercive leadership. To conclude, whether leadership is based on military or economic superiority (or superiority in some other value base), it can be coercive or noncoercive (or, in practice, of course, both at once).

Positive Sanctions

We have not yet mentioned a mode of power or influence which occurs frequently in international affairs and is especially important in a study of the political economy of power and influence. This is what is sometimes called "reward power" or "positive sanctions." It is the influence based on A's promise of some sort of goal gratification to B *on condition* that B will supply something of value to A. It occurs in a transaction that can be looked at as an exchange. For example, one state provides another with an air base in exchange for economic aid. A bribe is in the same category, since it is a prepaid reward.

Whether or not reward power is coercive is a key question in our context. Many writers hold the promise of reward to give rise to clearly noncoercive influence. This is no doubt correct under many circumstances. After all, B is presumably free to agree on any exchange of benefits. A "bought" an air base, and B "bought" economic aid. The *quid pro quo* implies that B will be no worse off, and presumably will be better off, *if* he responds to A's promise. The promise in such a proposed exchange is really a bid. Were he subject to coercion, B would be definitely worse off than before.

But even though calling the relationship noncoercive seems satisfactory in many conceivable situations, is it satisfactory in all? In some cases positive sanctions are used along with negative ones. A is threatening B but offers a reward as well with the expectation that, by reducing the latter's costs of compliance, he is more likely to get his way. For example, the reward may act as a "sweetener" or as a face-saving symbol. If the offer and acceptance of a reward is not a once-for-all or very occasional, but rather a frequent or regular, event, the recipient may become dependent on the reward, and the rewarding actor is setting up, or at any rate is presented with, a base for subsequent coercion. He can threaten to cut off the reward. And what if the promised reward is the suspension of a punishment? "The carrot or the stick" is a phrase suggesting an ambience palpably different from normal commercial exchanges. It suggests that the dispensing actor (e.g. the lord or boss) is manipulating the "donkey" (e.g. the peasant or lowly worker or slave), that the choice of either coercion or reward is strictly a matter of expedience, and that even if the carrot is chosen, the recipient is aware of the alternative of the stick. This kind of situation may come about even in the case of commercial exchanges. In the eyes of the economist, to be sure, exchange opportunities will be consummated only when they are perceived to be advantageous by the parties to the prospective trade. Neither the supplying nor the demanding party imposes his will on the other. Traders are neither malevolent nor benevolent. They simply look out for themselves. Thus, the economist ordinarily abstracts power or coercion from any realities. In certain areas, to be sure, he has felt obliged to take cognizance of the intrusion of power and coercion. He realizes that in other than perfectly competitive markets (i.e. where neither the individual seller nor the individual buyer has influence on price), there is apt to be conflict over the exchange ratio. He understands that the monopolist has market power and that, in the case of bilateral monopoly, bargaining outcomes hinge on the economic "power" of the parties (e.g. employers versus organized labor). He is also aware that many transactions in the real world are not exactly like the exchange of two commodities—for example, the labor contract, and that certain inequalities produced by some unregulated markets lead to "unjust" results that call for regulation (e.g. child labor). Socialists have pointed to other peculiarities of free markets. They observed that although the consumer is sovereign in a free market, the rich speak with greater authority of purse than the poor, that inequalities in the distribution of purchasing power are not only the just result of differential contributions to the productive process, and that taking wants as given, which is what economists do, ignores important parts of reality (which the economist admits but does not regard as *his* problem).

There is no question but that parties to exchange transactions may feel exploited. However, the subjective feeling of being exploited does not necessarily indicate the presence of coercion. Obviously, many traders would prefer a greater reward for what they sell or indeed a reward without any *quid pro quo* whatever. Yet they have to come to terms with the perennial fact of scarcity. Most valued things are more or less scarce, and there must be some sort of allocative mechanism for rationing them out. The market and bargaining are such distributive mechanisms.

Nevertheless, some situations of exchange do suggest exploitation by the normative standards of many communities. There are well-known cases of people who, under conditions of exceptional distress, have urgent and basic wants that can be used as leverage by others. There is the speculator in a backward country who hoards grain in anticipation of crop failure and famine and then sells food at prices requiring the starving poor to mortgage their property and future products; and there is the usurer who lends money to the unfortunate at exorbitant rates. There is the famous Biblical story of the famished Esau selling his birthright to Jacob for a mess of pottage; and there is the historical fact of widespread debt slavery. These situations are quite different from ordinary market transactions. They suggest that the possessor of a temporary advantage (which is not due to his productive effort) can convert it into a permanent one. This sort of situation is by no means unknown in the modern world. *B* may hate to give an air base to *A* but is in desperate (ultimately political) need of economic aid. In fact, ordinary social intercourse suggests that even a gift may have similar consequences. Often the benefactor is not a peer but a superior, and the recipient may feel constrained to show gratitude in various ways. Gifts may be a way of establishing superiority, and not rarely the recipient of a reward will feel degraded. An actor with ample resources enabling him to serve the urgent needs of others is in a position to capitalize on this and acquire power over them.

The conclusion is inescapable that some "power" to reward is susceptible to coercive exploitation. This is not the case in markets in which normal "exchangeables" of recognized suitability change hands on the basis of reciprocal intensity of demand, and which are characterized by a considerable number of competing buyers and sellers. (Competition always curtails power.)

Coercive potential is generated in exchange transactions if one or more of the following asymmetries characterize the relative bargaining positions of the actors. First, A has a substantial degree of monopoly power so that B cannot turn to alternative suppliers if he finds A's terms unacceptable. Second, A can bring into play coercive power, whether derived from military or economic power or some other power base, and thus reduces B's freedom to take or leave A's offer. (Western business enterprise dealing with authorities and landowners in undeveloped countries often enjoyed this advantage.) Third, A has superior market knowledge and is able to deceive B or to take advantage of his ignorance. Fourth, B's demand is inordinately intensive and inelastic because he has very little economic staying power when hit by an emergency beyond his control, such as war or a slump in his export markets. (This is the case of the famished peasant at a time of crop failure who sells his land for food to a usurious merchant.)

The concept of exploitation suggests that the outcome of a relationship or exchange is "unfair" or "unjust," that there is a lack of equivalence in the value of the things exchanged. It should be noted, however, that whether or not the outcome constitutes exploitation becomes a question of fact, capable of empirical verification, only with reference to a normative standard previously established. Moreover, the types of asymmetries between actors identified above do not produce exploitation *auto-*

matically. There is no law of nature making *A* grasping or malevolent. But history also reveals that the temptation of the strong, rich, and cunning to exploit the weak, poor, and ignorant is not easily resisted, within and between societies. The record also shows that, even when the temptation is resisted, the weak and destitute often suspect and allege exploitation. For these reasons, many societies lay down rules for curbing unequal power, even that of governments, and subject its use to legal and informal norms. But such laws and norms are largely absent from interstate relations, and those restraints that have recently evolved lack impartial enforceability.

The use of positive sanctions nevertheless differs from that of negative sanctions in important respects.[2] Promises are taken as a less unfriendly way of managing relationships than are threats. *B* feels less put upon and is less likely to defy the influence attempt. He receives something even if he also loses something of value. *B*'s relations with *A* are therefore less likely, in this case, to inhibit simultaneous co-operation on other matters or to leave a "scar effect" which limits or rules out friendly relations in the future than when he is subjected to a threat of deprivation of one kind or another. On the other side, the use of rewards not only requires "reward power"—the capability to promise worthwhile economic, diplomatic, or military benefits to B—but a successful attempt to influence the latter also results in corresponding costs to *A*. As we will examine in more detail below, the use of threats also involves costs. But the cost structure is different. Upon *B*'s compliance with a positive sanction, the reward is due, while nothing is due upon *B*'s compliance with a threat.

Power: Putative and Actualized

The phenomenon of power lends itself to two sharply different conceptions. The inability to grasp this difference leads to inevitable misunderstanding and confusion. Since coercive influence limits the conduct of an actor subjected to it, power can be seen to reside in the capabilities that permit the power-wielder to make effective threats. But it can also be seen as identical with, and limited to, the influence on the actually achieved behavior of the threatened actor. On the first view, power is something that powerful states have and can accumulate; power is a *means*. On the second view, power is an *effect*, that is the influence actually enjoyed. It is generated in an interaction which is an encounter. On the first view, power is something that an actor can hope to bring into play in a range of future situations. On the second, power comes into being, is shaped, and enjoyed only in a specific situation; its measure is the amount of influence actually achieved.

Today, most theorists conceive of power as actually achieved influence, whereas most laymen see it as reposing in the capabilities that permit strong threats to be made. Both concepts catch a part of reality. But it is critically important that we know which one we have in mind when we speak of "power." In the following, we will call the one *putative* power and the other *actualized* power. (When we refer simply to "power," the context makes it clear whether putative or actualized power is at issue.) The distinction is extremely important. Many people believe that armies and navies are military power, or that great national wealth is economic power, and they are inevitably puzzled when, in real life, superior national power so defined fails to coerce a weaker state, or when the superior power gets bested by an inferior one.

Having defined what actualized power is, we must now clarify what putative power consists of, and how it is converted into actualized power. We will do this in detail for military power and then more briefly for other types of coercive power and also for noncoercive influence.

Putative military power has three components: military forces, i.e. military strength; military potential, i.e. the capacity to expand or improve military forces; and military reputation, i.e. the expectation of other national actors, derived from past experience, that the state concerned has a greater or lesser disposition to resort to military threats when its vital interests are crossed.

There are three mechanisms through which military strength, or, more broadly, putative military power can become effective, that is, actualized. One is through war; the second is by way of military threats; and the third is through the anticipation or anxiety of other states that the nation involved may resort to its military force if a serious conflict of interest arises with them. This third mechanism is extremely important, even though it is the least noticeable, and is often expressed only in the councils of the influenced state but not always even there. For example, such councils may not consider certain courses of action at all because it is obvious to everyone that they are likely to incur the displeasure of a militarily very superior state; yet power has nonetheless become effective. Casting a quick glance at the historical record, it may appear to us that wars occur all too often. But it also tells us that they are the least frequent mechanism through which actualized power is achieved. Certainly, the use of threats is far more frequent; this follows logically from the fact that effective military threats do not lead to war and that not all ineffective threats do. Although the usually unobserved and often unobservable operation of the third mechanism denies us statistical evidence, it seems very likely that it is through this silent mechanism that putative military power is most often converted into actualized power. Governments do not like to incur coercive threats. The third mechanism of conversion has the further peculiarity that military power becomes effective without any encounter. If the "exercise" of power requires "manifest intention," [3] then this mechanism leads the strong state to enjoy the fruits of power without deliberately wielding it. In many instances, the powerful state may not even be aware of its power having become actualized.

But how exactly does putative military power become effective? What circumstances affect the transformation? The conversion process can be elucidated by the construction of conversion models, that is to say, by the identification of the main conditions which usually govern the transformation of putative power to actualized power. We will demonstrate a simple model involving military threats (letting the reader adapt the model to the other two mechanisms). The effectiveness of a military threat by A against B tends to depend upon the following factors:

1. B's estimate of the costs of complying with A's threat
2. B's estimate of the costs of defying A's threat
3. B's bargaining skill relative to A's
4. B's propensity to act rationally and to assume risks

To explain briefly, (1) B's estimate of the costs of compliance includes not only the value to him of the stake (whatever it is, e.g. territory) originally involved in the conflict with A, but also additional values that may come into play once a threat is received, e.g. the international loss of face, the domestic political weakening of B's government in the event of compliance. The higher the costs of compliance, the less likely B will yield to the threat. (2) B's estimate of the costs of defiance include its estimate that A will actually execute his threat if defied and the probable consequences, in the event the threat is executed, involving B's estimate of relative military capabilities, the losses suffered as a result of military destruction, the loss in his putative military power if defeated, the additional demands A may make if victorious, and the nature of domestic and foreign support in the event of military conflict. Clearly, the higher the estimated costs of defiance, the more likely B will comply. Since loss of face matters, B's cost of compliance is less when the threat is inferential rather than substantive. (3) The relative bargaining skill of the parties is important in that B, if he is a skillful bargainer, may protract negotiations, offer minimal concessions, make commitments which make compliance harder, or otherwise appear more determined to resist than he actually is, including perhaps a show of irrationality. In short, the more skillful B is, the less likely it is that A's threat will prevail. (4) Governments and nations differ in their disposition to act rationally and to assume risks. The more

B favors risk-taking the less likely he is to yield to *A*'s threat. And the less rational he is in making decisions in a crisis, the more likely he is to comply even where the estimated net costs of resistance favor defiance. And conversely, he may defy even when the estimated net costs of resistance are discouraging. Viewing a large number of military threats, it is a plausible hypothesis to assume that, in most instances, *B*'s net estimate (in terms of values and probabilities) of the costs of compliance and defiance will weigh more heavily than the other factors. This is likely to be so because intergovernmental differences in skill, rationality, and taking of risks are usually small. Therefore, unless there is evidence to the contrary in a particular case, one would predict that *B*'s estimate of net costs will be decisive.

This model, which could be made more complicated by the introduction of more differentiation in the identification of factors, makes it clear that a number of variable conditions intervene in determining whether a military threat will be effective. Superior military strength does not by itself assure conversion. If the costs of compliance are very high to *B,* if he has reason to anticipate the support of powerful allies, he may well defy the threat of a superior power. Even the military threat of a superior power may fail because its military strength is overextended in other conflicts, because a large part of its military strength is irrelevant to a particular situation (i.e. nuclear capabilities), because counterpower coalesces as other states come to the support of the threatened state, because the government loses its domestic support, etc.

Finally, the model assumes basically that *B* is rational. If he is definitely not, the results of threats are unpredictable since *B* may then make completely unrealistic estimates or refrain from making any estimates at all. Extreme irrationality can happen, but we regard it as a chance event since it is rare among modern governments that act through more or less elaborate bureaucracies. However, rational behavior is a question of more or less, not of either/or; and it is well known that governments (perhaps especially when acting through bureaucracies) do not act with perfect rationality. Crisis conditions often degrade rationality to some extent (as a result of time pressure, fatigue, anxiety, etc.). For such ordinary deviations from perfect rationality, we have made allowance in the model. There is, of course, the further and normal problem that, even though disposed to act rationally, governments may lack adequate information for making the estimates that underlie their decisions. Unquestionably, governments make errors, and some decisions to comply or to defy are apt to be mistaken. However, we have also assumed that governments know that their information is inadequate and will prudently take uncertainty into account.

It is possible, and often useful, to design similar models identifying the variables that will make A decide whether or not to make a threat (or whether to execute the threat when he has been defied). Regarding the initial decision, we may postulate that it depends mainly upon (1) A's estimate of the value to him of B's compliance, in terms of the values at stake in the original conflict, but possibly also in terms of the benefits of a successful threat in its effect on other states and for future power plays, and in terms of the government's position at home; (2) A's estimate of the diverse costs of making the threat, including any adverse reaction of opinion, both domestic and of other states, the various costs of being defied, and the costs involved in executing a defied threat; (3) A's propensity to act rationally and to assume risks.

The model can accommodate all possible decisions of this kind. For instance, it helps to explain why the United States, though overwhelmingly more powerful militarily, did not react with a forceful and explicit threat against North Korea when that small power seized the *Pueblo* in 1968. With so much of its military strength tied up in the Vietnamese war, the American public increasingly tired of that conflict, opinion elsewhere critical of United States military intervention abroad, and North Korea likely to receive Soviet and Chinese backing, the estimated costs of any specific threat loomed presumably very large in relation to any conceivable gain.

It is important to realize that attempts at achieving coercive influence involve costs. The extent to which power will be employed clearly depends on the sensitivity of the power holder to the costs of its use. J. Harsányi has suggested that a complete measure of A's actualized power depends upon the ratio of the cost of the power play to A and the costs of defiance to B. Accordingly, the more power A has, the less his costs and the higher the costs of resistance to B.[4] And power is more efficient as the value of the stakes at issue exceeds the costs incurred in wielding it. The transformation of putative into actualized power is obviously least costly, if costly at all, when the third conversion mechanism is operating. There is then no test of power which may fail and end up by diminishing A's putative power. And conversion is much less costly when a threat is effective than when the threat has to be made good. This cost is less or absent when the threat is inferential rather than substantive. If A's threat does not suffice to extract B's compliance, B is presumably testing A's putative power, and there is already a considerable loss in having one's power disputed, and perhaps revealed as pretended power. The need for excessive reliance on violence can be regarded as an index of weakness rather than of strength.[5] (Certainly, in domestic situations, violence tends to appear when power is in jeopardy.) And there is the additional cost that, once violence has begun, B's resistance may grow and a settlement by reconciliation and compromise is made more difficult.[6] It is for these reasons unwise for the threatening power to proceed automatically to violence when a military threat has been repudiated. There is usually ample cause for re-estimating the situation. Meeting a test of power may have harmful side effects when it occurs under circumstances so costly—for instance, as a consequence of domestic disunity—that its repetition will be doubted. On the other hand, A's coercive threat tends to be more effective, as B is surer that it will be executed in the event of noncompliance. And though power tests are costly, the avoidance of such tests may be interpreted as signifying fear and irresolution and may thus cause putative military power to suffer decline. Finally, even though the making and execution of threats is costly, the rewards may be high, not necessarily in terms of the issue at stake, but in terms of maintaining or enhancing a reputation for power which may lead to ready actualization in future conflicts or, hopefully, through the third mechanism. To set an example and to display military resolve is why governments have sometimes resorted to threats or to their execution, even though the precipitating cause of conflict seemed relatively unimportant.

The Effectiveness of Economic and Other Nonmilitary Power and Influence

Nonmilitary coercion and noncoercive influence are subject to the same kind of analysis we applied to military power. And so is the use of nonmilitary power in changing the *status quo* without influencing actors. Since much of this would be repetitive, we will examine these other forms of influence more briefly as far as the conversion process is concerned. Economic power with reference to coercive threats is used to deny some sort of economic advantage to another state, often but by no means necessarily always for the purpose of gaining some economic benefit. For instance, *A* may place an embargo on imports from *B* in order to compel *B* to change its political or economic behavior. The ability to shut off valuable markets, to pre-empt sources of supply, to stop investments, or reduce economic aid would constitute elements of national economic strength equivalent to military strength. The ability to increase such international economic control constitutes potential economic strength, and the known disposition to have recourse to economic pressures would be the remaining constituent of putative economic power. Clearly, the three conversion mechanisms will be operating with this form of power. A variety of factors intervenes to permit or deny, more or less, the transformation of economic power into effective influence over another actor's behavior. The expected costs to *A* of the economic threat, or of executing it, and the expected vulnerability of B to the threat, will figure eminently in A's decision. Expectations regarding domestic and foreign support will affect decisions. And again, the achievement of coercive influence will depend on B's calculations of the comparative costs of compliance or defiance and the degree of his disposition to act rationally and to take risks. In this area, too, the evaluation of threats and noncompliance are subject to misperception, and their effect is subject to change (e.g. a disastrous crop or prolonged major strikes in the threatened country). And the value of the stakes involved in the conflict affect B's decision to make or execute an economic threat and B's decision to cope with the threat or its execution. It is also clear that *effective* influence is achieved only in concrete situations.

If we turn to the promise of reward (whatever it be, e.g. military, economic, or diplomatic), the structure of factors involved in other coercive threats will be operative in those cases in which, for the reasons indicated in the foregoing, the carrot carries the suggestion of being a substitute for the stick. In other cases of a promise of goal gratification conditional on some *quid pro quo,* we have noncoercive influence aiming at the exchange of some sort of benefits. We have then a bargaining process free of coercion. Whether or not a reward will be offered or accepted depends on each party's estimate of whether the exchange is advantageous and also on the actors' estimate of whether the expected benefit will actually be forthcoming. The eventual settlement will reflect the bargaining power of the two parties which, tactical skills aside, favors the party that has the lesser perceived interest in reaching agreement.

Other Characteristics of Power and
Noncoercive Influence

In order to complete our analysis, we will set forth briefly a number of characteristics that all forms of influence more or less share.

The international power and noncoercive influence of states differ in amount or strength, that is to say in weight, scope, and domain.[7] Weight reflects the degree to which the policy of the influenced state is affected. Scope refers to the range of values in regard to which its behavior is influenced (e.g. it may be more influenceable in economic than military matters). Domain refers to the number of states that are being influenced. A state may succeed in coercing several others by the same threat or may persuade a number of them to co-operate with the same proposal. The influence relationship can be multilateral as well as bilateral. Indeed it can, and very often is, multilateral not only with reference to a single actor attempting to influence several others by means of the same threat, reward, or proposal, but also in terms of several actors attempting simultaneously to influence the same state or states. Whether coercive or not, the attempt at influence occurs frequently in a competitive situation. When actors attempt to exercise influence competitively, the actualization of their putative influence, whether coercive or not, tends to be diminished. Rivalry for influence is especially important in coercive situations, for it tends to limit the weight, scope, and domain of power. *B* may be able to play off one state against another. His will (and ability) to resist *A* may be abetted by *C*'s offer of backing (or, of course, by *C*'s threat against *A,* in which case power is directly limited by power). The influence relationship is modified further if several strong states combine to influence a weak one or if several weak states combine to defy, or perhaps even threaten, a strong one.

In our foregoing analysis, we assumed that influence is one-sided and that only one kind and means of influence is employed in any particular situation. We must now relax these and other simplifying assumptions. Coercive power, if it comes about, is of course inherently asymmetrical. But this does not mean that B, who is subjected to A's attempt to coerce, may not be able to exert counterinfluence in the process. If he is being threatened militarily, he may mobilize to suggest that he has the resolution to resist. Or he may negotiate for the support of other states. Indeed, as Boulding and Schelling have pointed out, the apparently weaker party may sometimes win because of superior determination, in turn resulting from the fact that its range of choice is more limited, or because choice has been limited by irrevocable commitment.[8] If power becomes actualized, it does so as a result of A's *net* ability to coerce. B may be able in various ways to raise A's costs in trying to actualize putative power. Indeed, actualization of power will proceed only and precisely as far as B's resistance permits.

To lift another simplifying assumption, an attempt at coercion may not only flatly fail or succeed. It may succeed (or fail) in part, namely to the extent set by B's will and ability to resist. Indeed, if we conceive of the value X that A wants to extract from B as something divisible (which it may or may not be), we can hypothesize that A's resistance to further losses will grow progressively with each unit of X given up, while A's will to pay the costs and assume the risks of power conversion will decline with each unit of X gained. (In real life, the problem may not, of course, be a linear one.) The outcome will then represent a compromise.

The bargaining involved in attempts at coercion is frequently protracted. B's skill may make it so. This means that the variable conditions determining the conversion of putative into actualized power may change during the time of the bargaining process. A may suddenly find a part of his putative power claimed by conflicts with other states; B may come to enjoy increasing domestic or foreign support, etc. On the other hand, there may be changes to B's disadvantage. Such changes will induce the actors to reconsider and perhaps revise earlier decisions to inflict or resist coercion. As a result, *B*'s resistance may crumble or mount, or *A*'s position may be strengthened or weakened.

In our simple model, we also assumed that only one base or means of influence was operating at any one time. In the real world, *A* may resort to several different threats (i.e., a threat package) and *B* to several different counterthreats. Thus, *A* may threaten *B* with economic reprisals and promise to reward *B* with certain economic advantages, while *B* may counter with a propaganda campaign directed at *A*'s public. Since states may find it to their mutual advantage to engage in limited co-operation even in the midst of a serious crisis (or war), noncoercive influence may be intermixed with attempts at coercion. The ability to act as an international leader may likewise rest on a blending of coercive and noncoercive influence. Or in the complete absence of coercion, a state may lead on the basis of several shared values, e.g., information, expertise, and trust. If a particular encounter allows a rational leader to choose from several available means of influence, he will compare their expected costs and effectiveness and then combine them in such a way as to achieve a particular effect at minimum cost and risk.

The choice of means, however, depends not only on their availability to government and on the expected cost and efficacy of their employment. It depends also on the character of past relationships between states. Previous relationships and hence predispositions may be of long-standing friendship or hatred, trust or suspicion, confidence or fear; and these attitudes condition both the generation and resolution of conflict and the scope for noncoercive influence. Prior amity will tend to minimize the very generation of conflict, at least serious conflict (though by no means prevent it), since governments and publics are disposed to be accommodating. When conflicts do arise, attempts at pacific settlement have priority. Resort to coercion is shunned as inappropriate, and will be considered only when the stakes are extremely high. An established friendly relationship obviously facilitates co-operation and the mutual flow of noncoercive influence. Conversely, conflicts are apt to arise more easily and attempts at coercion are considered more readily within a relationship of antagonism.

Special relationships may be based on a long history of cooperation and alliance, or on a common culture and language, or —less solidly—on close economic ties. They produce a context which, affecting the choice of influence attempts, is expressed in the very tone of diplomacy, in a distinct ambiance. During the 1960's, for example, the tone of American diplomacy vis-à-vis Russia and China was suspicious, cool, and sometimes frosty, while that exhibited in American relations with England and Japan was more often confident and friendly.

International Power and Influence Structures

Viewing international systems as a whole—whether global as now or regionally confined as before the overseas eruption of European power—the distribution of putative power and influence and the foundations on which they rest have shown various patterns, the only uniform property being the inequality of the units. Depending on the base value from which international power and influence are derived, one could identify a number of not wholly overlapping patterns at any one time. The dominant pattern has thus far always been founded on military and economic strength. Since noncoercive as well as coercive influence can turn on these very same assets, and since some other assets are usually associated with economic power (e.g. wide-ranging expertise), the international pattern of noncoercive influence has tended to gravitate toward the pattern of coercive power. There are, however, influence bases which need not be associated with military and economic strength, such as certain bargaining skills, the image of a successful mastery of domestic problems, cultural affinity, and ethnic identity.

Looked at from the viewpoint of the majority of small and weak states—and the international system looks immensely different from the vantage point of Manila, San Salvador, or Copenhagen than from that of Washington, Moscow, or Peking—the system is one of limited international freedom of action and decidedly little security from aggression.[9] To the extent that goal achievement requires external power, they have fewer feasible options than the strong; and their usually narrow margin of safety is highly demanding of vigilant prudence. (Only the strong can hope somehow to "muddle through.") According to their experience as a group, the international balance of power and the bipolar systems are designed primarily to promote the interests of the great or of the superpowers respectively. Faced with these prospects, some small states have embraced neutralism or nonalignment; others tried appeasement of the most threatening power. Alternatively, the weak state may seek protection in alliance with a strong power—a time-honored practice—or, more recently, in systems of collective security. Yet, whatever alternative they turn to, they depend for their security ultimately on external assistance or luck. They cannot assure it from their own resources. There are, as we shall see, some changes in the contemporary world that have somewhat eroded the military foundation of power, but essentially the international system is still one of basic insecurity for the weak.

Looked at from the viewpoint of the strong state, the systems have actually been only relatively more secure for them than for the weak, when (and this is the rule) there was one other power, or more powers, of comparable strength. Anarchy, though it gives predatory opportunities to the strong, is a risk and a burden to all members. Yet despite this inescapable fundamental insecurity, strong states of course enjoyed opportunities (while they lasted) for pushing their goal achievement at the expense of the small fry (and hence have been far less stimulated than lesser states to revolutionize the international system in the direction of viable collective security).

Unequal putative power facilitates the establishment of empire, including colonial empire in which the colonial population, with lesser rights than the imperial population, is subject to exploitation. Unequal power also facilitates the establishment and preservation of a range of national privileges, diplomatic and economic, which are not expressed in territorial control. Unequal power, furthermore, favors hegemony, which, without formal institutionalization of authority, means supremacy in an area that the hegemonical state controls fundamentally by coercive power. (Noncoercive influence, no matter how one-sided, can bring about leadership but not hegemonical supremacy.) The lesser states within the sphere of influence of the hegemonical state—a sphere often tacitly recognized by other strong states, usually on the expectations that other powerful states will reciprocate by similarly acknowledging *their* sphere of interest—are essentially satellites. Unlike colonial dependencies or protectorates, they retain formal sovereignty but in important foreign-policy respects they lack autonomy—not only on the essentially *ad hoc* basis on which weak states see their self-determination episodically restricted by more powerful states, but on a regular basis. There can be little doubt about the Soviet Union's hegemonic power over the Communist states in Eastern Europe, except Yugoslavia and Albania, even though there have been attempts from time to time by the smaller Communist states to contest and reduce the scope of Soviet hegemony. Rumania's strivings in the middle and late 1960's are a case in point.

Another relationship resting on inequality of power and influence is patronal leadership.[10] If as ideal types (reality is messy!), empire means formal subjection to a central authority (i.e. the imperial state alone has formal sovereignty), and hegemony is coercive domination over formally independent units, then patronal leadership is based on a mixture of coercive and noncoercive influence, with noncoercive influence and noncoercive bargaining, not an incidental or marginal admixture, but a very important—often an equal or a predominant—foundation of the relationship. The patronal leader occupies internationally a position similar to ruling elites within relatively nonautocratic states. Such elites organize and finance, by means of taxes and other extractions from the rest of the populations (e.g. military conscription) the production of public goods and services (e.g. domestic order and school systems), which would not be produced or paid for voluntarily. These elites enjoy their position by a varying combination of coercion and consent. Internationally, the patronal leader organizes the achievement of some sort of net benefits to himself and his client state or client states. (The "public" benefits may involve military protection by means of alliance, the support of friendly foreign governments challenged by revolutionaries, or the formation of a customs union [as did Prussia in the 1830's]). Or the benefits may be directed to a range of common problems, as is the case with the Organization of American States, for which the United States acts as patronal leader. Patronal leadership may also be multilateral—for instance, the leadership of the "Big Four" in the establishment of the United Nations at the end of World War II and the United States and Great Britain in the creation of the International Monetary Fund and the International Bank for Reconstruction and Development. On the other hand, when the United States proposed and financed the Marshall Plan for the economic reconstruction of war-torn Europe, it acted as a single patron.

Domestic elites may use their authority to extract resources for the provision of public goods in order to exploit the rest of the population by means of excessive taxation or by defining as "public" goods those in which only they are primarily interested (e.g. an ambitious buildup of military strength). Similarly, the patronal leader may exploit his international clients by extracting advantages redounding only or mainly to his interests. Thus, an alliance leader may use military bases supplied by smaller allies for operations that have nothing to do with alliance business and which these allies may sense as disadvantageous to themselves. However, the examples we have given do not indicate that patronal leaders will often be in a position to exploit their clients on a net basis. What happens in this respect depends primarily on whether the leader enjoys appreciable net coercive power or whether he leads on the basis of noncoercive influence and the exchange of *quid pro quo*s. It is quite possible for a client to exploit the patronal leader if he has adequate bargaining power. For instance, he may threaten to switch to a rival leader or collapse against the pressure of domestic revolutionary forces under circumstances which make his survival and that of the client relationship very desirable to the patronal leader. Thus, it is quite likely that some postwar clients of the United States (e.g. the Republic of China on Taiwan or South Korea) have exploited the United States. Indeed, there has been speculation on whether the United States has not been exploited by some of its NATO allies who supplied far smaller inputs for alliance purposes than the United States had requested or suggested or even than they had agreed to provide. And it is quite possible that Communist China exploited the Soviet Union before the rift between the two states opened and expanded sharply in 1963.

It hardly needs emphasizing that, in the real world, mixed relationships frequently occur. Elements of empire and/or hegemony may be associated with elements of patronal leadership. For example, although the sway of the Soviet Union over most of the Eastern European countries has a definite hegemonical basis, as the occupation of Czechoslovakia in 1968 manifested clearly, there are also elements of patronal leadership in the sense that the governments of the smaller countries regard Russia as a guarantor of security from external aggression, a guarantor perhaps also of their own national rule, and an international leader in the promotion of Communism.

Notes

1. Carl J. Friedrich, *Man and His Government* (New York: McGraw Hill, 1963), p. 168.

2. David A. Baldwin, "The Power of Positive Sanctions," *World Politics* 24 (1971): 19–38.

3. Robert A. Dahl, "Power," *International Encyclopedia of the Social Sciences*, vol. 12 (New York: Macmillan, 1968), pp. 412–413.

4. J. Harsányi, "Measurement of Social Power," *Game Theory and*

Related Approaches to Social Behavior, ed. Martin Shubik (New York: Wiley, 1964), pp. 186–188.

5. Harold D. Lasswell and Abraham Kaplan, *Power and Society* (New Haven: Yale University Press, 1950), p. 266.

6. Kenneth E. Boulding, *Conflict and Defense, A General Theory* (New York: Harper, 1962), p. 323.

7. Lasswell and Kaplan, *Power and Society,* pp. 73–77.

8. Boulding, *Conflict and Defense,* p. 254; Thomas C. Schelling, *Arms and Influence* (New Haven: Yale University Press, 1966), chap. II.

9. Cf. Robert L. Rothstein, *Alliances and Small Powers* (New York: Columbia University Press, 1968), esp. chap. I.

10. Gerald Garvey, "The Political Economy of Patronal Group," *Public Choice* I (Winter 1970): 34.

CHAPTER

2

Foreign Policy and National Interest

This book is concerned with foreign policy, that is to say, with the use of different resources by states for achieving various kinds of gain in their relations with other states. Attention will be paid both to noneconomic foreign policy which primarily involves action designed to relate national purposes to the foreign political and military environment, and economic foreign policy which, in the main, serves the same function regarding the international economic environment. Analytically speaking, governments employ political and military means toward achieving economic as well as political and military ends; and they use economic means toward serving political and military as well as economic ends. Our principal focus is on these interrelationships.

However, the complexity of this subject matter is increased further by the fact that foreign and domestic policies and politics are closely linked. Thus foreign economic policy may be employed as a means of national economic policy in countering deflation or promoting economic growth. Or it may be used as a means, as in the case of tariff protection, of maintaining privileged access to income of the influential owners of certain assets (e.g. wheat producers in West Germany and sugar producers in the United

States). Similarly, noneconomic foreign policy may serve the purpose of increasing national solidarity in a politically divided community.

Before beginning with the analysis presented in subsequent chapters, we must therefore first elucidate, though briefly and selectively, some of the conditions underlying these complex relationships. We must ask the following questions: how are international relations related to the goals of societies, and what is the function of foreign (and military) policy from this point of view? By which processes are the purposes of foreign policy determined, the national interest defined, and various resources allocated in support of these purposes? What is the nature, and which are the conditions of rationality in the making of foreign policy? And which conditions cause deviations from rational behavior? These questions are explored in the remainder of this chapter.

This focus on government policy excludes from major consideration those kinds of international relations which occur between private groups and individuals across national boundaries. Many of these interactions are fostered by governments, as for instance is international trade, and their regulation often raises issues of foreign policy. In some cases, as for example with the so-called "multinational" business corporations, governments have encountered difficulties in controlling activities which conflict with government policy.

Abstractly considered, every society organized in a sovereign state uses various inputs (e.g. labor, capital, knowledge) for producing a variety of material and nonmaterial values—such as physical security, consumers' goods, education, political participation, foreign policies—and distributes them or their results, for consumption or as means to other ends, to its members. Political and economic systems are social arrangements by which the supply of inputs, the organization of the production process, and the distribution of outputs are regulated. The composition of value output depends on the structure of effective demand for various values. Effective demand is a function of both the distribution of value preferences in society and the relative strength with which individuals and groups are able and determined to exert their preferences, whether by means of purchasing power or various types of influence. The ability to make demand effective as well as the eventual distribution of the output is determined primarily by differences in power and influence, wealth, and income among members of society.

Foreign Policy: Nature and Purpose

International transactions serve to relate each society's production and consumption of values to that of other societies organized as states. The extent to which the value production and consumption of states are interdependent is affected by technology, i.e. the feasibility and costs of international transportation and communication, and depends otherwise on the policies of states. Co-operation and conflict are modes of interaction that tend to increase international interdependence. On the one hand, societies co-operate in order to augment the production of values available to each. They are in that case pursuing compatible goals. All the participating societies gain. International trade and organized peace are examples of such co-operation. On the other hand, societies fight in order to gain, or keep from losing, value outputs or inputs required for the production of values. In such cases, they are pursuing incompatible goals. If A gains, he does so at the expense of B. Territorial conquest is a way to incorporating foreign inputs of labor and natural resources. Domination is a way to taxing the value output of other societies. International co-operation and conflict are frequently related, since societies may conflict on the distribution of the value increments created by international co-operation. By means of international co-operation or conflict, then, each state attempts to enrich the goal achievement of society subject to foreign and national restraints.

The foreign policies of states are actions, or strategies for action, on the part of their governments designed to terminate, reduce, sustain, or expand co-operation and conflict. When foreign policies are conflictive, they can be more or less aggressive or defensive. When they are conflictive or co-operative, they can be more or less active or passive, and more or less initiatory or reactive. Looked at from a different viewpoint, the foreign policies of societies are attempts either at adapting their goals to other external environment or at adapting environment to their goals. In the pursuit of these effects, foreign policies relate means to ends. The means are not necessarily material. In order to lower or raise barriers to foreign trade, a government needs only sufficient domestic support. In order to take the lead in organizing new co-operative ventures, its diplomacy needs to be guided by attractive ideas. However, a wide range of foreign policies call for material resources: for instance, the use of military strength or the extension of foreign loans clearly do so. Even to maintain accredited representatives abroad is no small matter for some of the tiny states. To the extent that foreign policy is rational, ends must be balanced by sufficient means. Goals will be frustrated if they lack adequate resources to be employed in conflict or for co-operation.

The values that governments seek to augment or protect through international action are of many kinds: political, economic, cultural, etc. Their composition will be determined by two conditions, one on the demand, and one on the supply side. First, values are demanded by members of society, and tend to be ranked in terms of marginal preference or utility. Second, there is the opportunity to secure these values by international action either because they are incapable of being produced at home or because—on the basis of comparative-production costs—they can be acquired, wholly or in part, more cheaply through international transactions. Economists have demonstrated this logic in matters of international trade and investment. Thus, goods are

imported, usually in exchange for exports, either because resources for their domestic production do not exist, or do not exist
in sufficient quantity, or because the cost of imports is smaller
than the cost of domestic output. The same logic applies to
obtaining other, nonmaterial values, e.g. political self-preserva-
tion, the reputation of leaders, the urge to dominate, etc. For
example, the urge to rule or to spread an ideology, and to increase the number of the ruled or of the converts, may point to
external conquest or conversion.

To the extent that the preference functions of society are thus
interdependent, in protecting values, foreign policy is a reaction
to external challenges; and in increasing the supply of values,
foreign policy is a reaction to opportunities perceived in the
outside world. Most outward-reaching foreign policy is not a
matter of detailed, long-run plans, but, in a continuously changing world, is rather opportunistic. National interests and foreign opportunities are thus interdependent. National interest in-
spires governments to be alert to opportunities for serving them
internationally. Interest becomes concrete in foreign-policy objectives when opportunity is recognized and evaluated as worth
pursuing, in terms of expected costs, in particular contexts. These
relationships make it clear that foreign-policy objectives are
inconstant. The national structure of demand for values, comparative costs in supplying these values abroad or at home, and
foreign threats to a society's value achievement are subject to
change, and, especially in the contemporary world, in continuous flux.

There is one particular value that demands singling out
because it plays a crucial role in the international goal striving of
states. This is putative power and influence over other states. International power is obviously instrumental to protecting and increasing a society's supply of many other values. This fact tends
to dispose governments, more or less, to build up putative power
for future use when external challenges or opportunities arise.
They tend to do so for two reasons. First, the production and

accumulation of international power is time-consuming. To achieve industrial development or to increase armed forces, or to cultivate an international reputation for exercising power when important interests are at stake, takes substantial time. On the other hand, secondly, foreign challenges and opportunities are likely to arise suddenly. Their future occurrence is impossible to predict with any confidence. Obviously, since the generation of many forms of putative power is expensive (values, such as manpower and other resources, are absorbed in its production), it would be efficient to produce putative power only when the need is acute, to produce it only in the form in which it is needed, and only in the amount required. But the lengthy time lag involved in generating power, and the difficulty of predicting the need for it, support the option of producing a degree of power to cover unknown contingencies and of mobilizing more putative power as the concrete need occurs.

There are, in fact, several incentives which limit the production of putative power for unknown future uses. First, the generation of such power is costly. Second, its utility in unknown future situations is subject to discount. The problem is therefore one of trade-offs, of finding an optimum solution, and not of maximizing putative power. There is indeed a third reason which tends to limit the accumulation of putative power. Interstate power is clearly relative. If A builds up power and is suspected by other governments of possibly employing it aggressively on future occasions, other states have an interest in building up counterpower. This is in fact how the balance of power operates. To the extent that this happens, A's attempt at accumulating power becomes ineffective. Part or all of the power build-up is negated by counterpower, and the resources for producing it have been wasted. For instance, this restraint operates, or will operate as long as governments act rationally, with reference to national security. Some provision for purposes of deterrence and defense in unknown future contingencies may be most sensible, if not indispensable. However, if military strength continues to be increased, and alliances formed or enlarged, other governments, also unable to predict future events, may become alarmed, fear for their own security, and expand their military preparations. To the extent that such an arms race is touched off, a part of the first state's attempt to provide for its security is negated since its security needs have now risen. It would have been better off if it had stopped at a less provocative level of preparedness.

The Determination of National Interest

But who fixes foreign policy, its content and character? How is the preference function of states in interstate affairs determined? To say that "national interests" do, explains nothing. What determines national interests? As it does with reference to value production in general, effective demands brought to bear on policy formulation define the national interests that governments, acting rationally, pursue. Since demands frequently conflict, foreign policy tends to represent the demands of the most influential coalition of particular interests. It is misleading to insist that, in addition to serving particular interests, governments also uphold basic national interests or "national welfare" in any way that transcends particularist demands. Of course, members of the government or public may see themselves, wholly or in part, in the role of trustees of the entire society making demands on foreign policy which they believe to reflect the larger interest associated with this role. In this case, the demands involved are nevertheless interests of the particular persons or groups concerned; and the demands of such groups, like consciously sectional demands, may not converge, since opinions differ on what the national interest is or on how to serve it.

To deny that there are transcendent and presumably enduring national interests is not saying that certain objectives relating to the external world may not be subscribed to by a large majority of the elite or of society as a whole. Security from foreign aggression is normally such a widely shared goal, and usually attracts wider support than any other goal of foreign policy. This is so because it represents a perceived self-interest that many, though not necessarily all, persons share.

If the national interest reflects the sum of separate interests, it is clear that the foreign policies of states do not necessarily—in fact usually do not—reflect exactly the national interest as defined. This is so for two reasons. First, only a fraction of the population participates in determining foreign policy and those who do participate have unequal influence. Second, to the extent that the interests of the participants conflict, they compete with each other, and foreign policy will serve only the perceived interest of those who win out in the competitive process.

The pattern of participation is only in part a function of formal political constitution. In principle, to be sure, more people are formally enabled to participate and compete under a democratic regime than in a formally authoritarian system. There are, however, other factors involved. The actual structure of power and influence usually deviates more or less from the formal structuring. People with equal rights enjoy vastly differing degrees of influence owing to variations in wealth and social position, education and skill, and personal ambition and concentration of effort. Whatever the formal rights or actual influence positions citizens or subjects have, their participation in defining national interests depends on the exercise, with more or less devotion, of the influence potential they have. Even in formally democratic states, the majority of citizens is, except in painful crisis situations, inert rather than alert when it comes to foreign-policy problems, leaving the definition of national interest normally to officialdom and a minority of citizens who, recruited chiefly from elite and middle-class layers, take a more frequent or continuous interest in these matters of state.

Whatever the political system, governments—which means people formally charged with formulating the foreign policy of states—are themselves an interest group (or a complex of interest groups) placed in a favorable position for defining the national interest. Usually, governments have a degree of autonomy for bringing influence to bear. Depending on their power and aspirations, leaders can use foreign policy for their own, essentially private, purposes. These purposes may be outward-directed, as when leaders crave world recognition or want to influence the external environment for other personal reasons. Or these purposes may be inward-directed, as when governments use foreign policy in order to prolong their tenure or otherwise increase their domestic power. Of course, governments are never completely united, and often far from unitary. This condition is important for, as will be pointed out below, it affects the efficiency and rationality as well as the goals of foreign policy. In this respect, moreover, the instrumental bureaucracies of government, including the armed services, grown enormously in size and complexity in modern states, act as additional sources of influence on the definition of national interest. Their function, in policy-setting and in policy-execution, places them in a strategic position for influencing the definition of the national interest. These bodies, and competing groups within them, act in their own interest as well as in the role to which they are formally appointed, whatever these special interests are, such as achieving more influence vis-à-vis other bureaucracies, expansion of personnel, a larger share of public revenues, and resistance to the pains of policy change imposed from outside. To the extent that bureaucratic groups, which are meant to be nothing but instruments, are enabled to engage in self-protection and self-aggrandizement, they distort the formulation and conduct of foreign and military policy.

The Supply of Foreign-Policy Resources

Since feasible goals of foreign policy must be matched by appropriate resources, many of which are material in character, the balance between demands on foreign policy and resource supplies to foreign policy is obviously a critical factor. This supply will take such forms as funds and manpower for military forces, goods to be shipped abroad as aid, and technical experts to serve as agents of intelligence. The volume and quality of resources mobilized for use in foreign affairs depends on two factors: first, the productive capacity and wealth of the country, i.e. manpower, capital, and land, and second, the share of these resources, or their outputs, allocated to foreign policy. This allocation results from the ability of government to extract appropriate inputs, diverting them from alternative uses, by means of requisitioning (e.g. drafting of military manpower) and of purchase, the rate of extraction being in turn a function of the government's authority to requisition and secure finance by taxation or borrowing.

Members of society act in the dual role of providing inputs for foreign policy and of making demands on it. The less the ability of government to extract resources for foreign policy is a matter of command, the more, in other words, it flows from the consent of the governed, be they few or many, the more directly are the demands on foreign-policy outputs linked to the supply of resource inputs, the more must government demonstrate that the required inputs are a necessary means to the achievement of specific goals of interest to those able to withhold or grant substantial resources. Influence over the supply of resources for foreign policy normally parallels the structure of influence in making effective demands on foreign policy. This holds true with reference to informal as well as formal structure as, for example, when democratic societies let their "establishment" make the effective demands on output and extract the inputs. On the other hand, it must be understood that elite groups or larger publics which lose out in the competition for influencing foreign and military policy are nevertheless unable to withhold resource inputs which are not voluntary. The pacifist as well as the militarist pays taxes from which military expenditures are derived. This effect obtains generally with the supply of public (or collective) goods; and the provision of government and of governmental policies must be regarded as a public good as much as the provision of public health and education or of religious symbols.

The production of public goods is organized by collective decision because, since in the nature of the case no charge can be made for consumption by individuals, voluntary contributions would fail to pay for their production. Inevitably, some members of society will pay more for the production of public goods, normally by means of taxes, or by being drafted for military service, than these goods are worth to them, while other individuals derive more value from their consumption than they pay. In fact, members will pay, even though they care nothing for a particular collective good or are strongly opposed to its production. Throughout history, rulers or ruling groups have been in a position to organize the production of public goods and determine their nature while imposing all or most of the costs of production on the public at large. Ruling groups may, of course, provide for public goods, in part at least, in response to the wants of the entire population. However, they are in a position to favor their own demands, whether or not they persuade the larger public that it also wants, or should want, the collective good in question. To the extent the public is made to pay for public goods it does not care about, it may or may not, objectively speaking, receive an equivalent return for the burden imposed on it. Whether or not it does depends on whether it would want the public good provided it possessed the resources, notably full information, to make an enlightened choice. The question of exploitation by ruling groups arises only if an enlightened choice would still lead the public to reject the public good concerned. This is an important consideration bearing on the value of foreign and military policy. Beyond doubt, many ruling groups have traditionally taken a special interest in foreign and military policy as a means to the enjoyment of expected benefits to themselves, and have imposed the costs on their societies. They are often in a position to extract most of the gains derived from an active foreign policy and to shift most of the costs to the rest of the population.

Rationality and Foreign Policy

Foreign and military policy, it has been demonstrated, are means employed in attaining the international goals of societies, and sometimes also in the domestic goals of their members. In the theory of choosing a policy and pursuing it, the actors are usually assumed to be rational. Since this assumption will also be made in much of the following analysis, it is imperative to be clear about the meaning and conditions of rational action, and also about deviations from such action and their conditions and consequences. Many conditions can degrade rationality, that is, the choice of action which maximizes the total value position of the actor. Some of these have been discussed in Chapter 1. Two more demand acknowledgment in the context of the making of foreign policy.

First, there are several factors which operate to obstruct consideration of a complete range of choices.[1] Defective knowledge about the environment is one condition that bounds rationality. Time pressures and fatigue can be another. A third factor is the limited capacity of any organization for formulating and solving complex problems. Basic ideological beliefs, for instance, Marxism, act as a fourth by constraining perceptions and filtering information. Operational assumptions, without which organizations can hardly work in a co-ordinated fashion, such as the "Cold War" assumptions of American officials in the 1950's and 1960's, have similar consequences, partly by being subject to unrecognized obsolescence. The last two factors especially tend to make the actor's mapping of the environment inevitably subjective. His subjective environment will coincide only more or less with the objective environment which will, however, determine the consequences, including success or failure, of the actor's choice.

The other major impediment to rational choice results from the fact that foreign policy is made not by one unitary actor but by several or many whose evaluations are affected both by the official role they play and by the personal interests they perceive to be at stake. Disagreement between top leaders, for instance between legislative and executive, can obviously hamstring the making of decisions. In addition to, and often through, their sensitivity to personal concerns, political leaders are subject to the pressure of interest groups. The top policy-makers must aggregate their demands, which are more or less inconsistent, vary in the political weight attached to them, and are often difficult to reconcile with external exigencies and with the supply of resource inputs. It is after all through these pulls and pushes that the weight of prospective policy gains and costs is registered and brought to bear on the articulation of foreign policy. As discussed in the foregoing, on a level below the leadership, the interests of bureaucracies themselves are apt to be divided in outlook and interests; likewise, they impinge on the making and execution of policy, often giving way to inertia, insisting on routine responses of a limited repertoire of processed policy devices, and pursuing parochial interests.[2]

Notes

1. H. A. Simon, *Models of Man* (New York: Wiley, 1957), pp. 196–206, 241–256.

2. Cf. Graham T. Allison, "Conceptual Models and the Cuban Missile Crisis," *The American Political Science Review* 63 (Sept. 1969): 689–718.

CHAPTER

3

The Bases of Military Power

In clarifying the bases of national military power, the chief focus of this study is on economic strength. The analysis of economic strength as a foundation of military strength will be followed by a somewhat shorter examination of the noneconomic foundations of military power. One cannot fully appreciate the importance of the economic bases without comparing them with noneconomic sinews of strength and without pointing up the principal interrelations between economic and noneconomic factors.

We will first turn to the determinants of putative military power—a concept elaborated in Chapter 1. The conversion of putative into actualized military power will receive attention in Chapter 5. To recall, the putative military power of states has three components: ready military forces, military potential (from which additional military capabilities can be derived), and military reputation, that is, the known and expected disposition of a society to resort to military strength if national interests are crossed by other societies, and its government decides to act.

Economic strength is a basis of two of these determinants, namely, mobilized forces and military potential. The base of economic strength has historically always been important in the relative military strength of organized communities. But the spread of interstate differences in economic wealth—per head of the population—has become far greater since the beginning of the industrial revolution than it was before. This follows simply from the fact that differences in per capita wealth have increased as some societies industrialized progressively while others remained at a preindustrial level of technology or managed only a low and fragmentary level of industrial development. As a consequence, one would deduce that the economic factor has acquired more impact, relative to other sources of military strength, in determining the comparative military power of states.

A state's economic strength [1] equals the productive resources that society controls: labor; technology; natural resources; real capital (in the form of factories, power dams, railroads, inventories of materials and manufactures, etc.); and claims on the real output of other societies in the form of reserves of international liquidity (gold, foreign currencies) and foreign investments. The study of economic strength must be approached both from the viewpoint of the magnitude of over-all production capacity and from that of the qualitative structure of this capacity. The first perspective leads to a comparison of aggregate output and income, the second to that of particular kinds of economic and technological capabilities.

The National Product and Its Uses

Not all of the productive capacity of states is, of course, available for the generation of military strength, since a large proportion is needed for, and allocated to, other purposes. At the height of their effort during World War II, Great Britain and Germany devoted about one-half of their economic strength, an extremely large proportion, to the waging of war. The fraction allotted to the military sector of contemporary societies is normally appreciably smaller. Taking the percentage of gross national product

(GNP) absorbed by a state's military effort as an approximate measurement of this proportion, it has fluctuated around 9 per cent in the United States during the 1950's and 1960's. In 1967, world military expenditures were estimated at 7.3 per cent of a world GNP of $2,482 million.[2] It ran higher in countries involved in or fearful of a military confrontation with another country or countries. Thus, it was then 10.7 per cent in Israel, 11.7 per cent in the United Arab Republic, and 25.0 per cent in North Vietnam. On the other hand, it was lower in countries feeling secure; e.g. it was 1.7 per cent in Colombia, 1.8 per cent in Ceylon, and 2.7 per cent in Denmark.

Statistics indicate a close relationship between GNP and military expenditures. In 1967, the ten countries ranking first in economic output, in descending order, were the United States, the Soviet Union, West Germany, France, Japan, the United Kingdom, China, Italy, Canada, and India. Together they produced 76 per cent of world GNP and accounted for 87 per cent of world military expenditures. All economically developed countries, small and large, produced 83 per cent of world GNP and accounted for 70 per cent of world military spending. The United States and the Soviet Union together contributed nearly half to total world production and 70 per cent to world military outlays. On the basis of military spending, the United States and the Soviet Union, the military superpowers, are clearly in a class by themselves. The Soviet Union, which ranks second in military outlays, spent almost nine times as much as France, whose spending was the third largest in the world. France, West Germany, the United Kingdom, Italy, China, and India may be regarded as middle powers. Since GNP reflects size of population and stage of economic development (as indicated by GNP per capita), some countries of large population (e.g. China and India) produce large GNP's and have large military expenditures, even though they are comparatively underdeveloped economically and poor, while other countries of moderate population size (e.g. West Germany and France) rank high in GNP and military outlays because they are highly developed economically and rich.

The GNP statistics are the only data permitting an international comparison of the economic capabilities of countries. The GNP is, however, a very rough, and far from accurate, indicator; and quantitative comparison encounters several conceptual and statistical difficulties. Its results should be accepted only with caution and reservation.[3] In the absence of better indicators, they are, nevertheless, worth studying.

When a foreign threat, an arms race, or war induces governments to expand military spending, causing it to rise as a percentage of GNP, other uses—private and public domestic consumption and investment, and net exports (or imports)—must decline proportionally. They must decrease in absolute amount unless rising allocations to the military sector can be afforded from an increase in GNP. The sources from which production resources can be extracted for the military sector can be summarized as follows:

	(1)	Gross National Product Prior to Increase in Military Demand
plus	(2)	Output of Productive Reserves or Natural Additions to the Labor Force
minus	(3)	Reduced Civilian Consumption
minus	(4)	Reduced Gross Domestic Investment
minus	(5)	Reduced Nonmilitary Purchases of Government
minus or plus	(6)	Change in Net Foreign Investment
minus or plus	(7)	Change in Labor Productivity
equals	(8)	Disposable Surplus for Military Sector

The opportunity costs of generating and employing military power equal the alternative uses of a stationary or expanding productive capacity which have been foregone. A large GNP indicates a natural ability to support a large military effort. It is therefore one determinant of economic military potential. Other factors being the same, a country devoting 10 per cent of its GNP to the military sector can be a match for one with a GNP twice as large but allocating only 5 per cent to military purposes. Whether or to what extent this potential is mobilized is, of course, a political question.

The rate at which national economies expand, which varies over time, is clearly significant from this point of view. If the American GNP at $1,000 billion grows, in real rather than monetary terms, at 4 per cent rather than 2 per cent per annum, the indicated difference in cumulative additions to productive power is appreciable. However, international differences in growth rates are significant relative to the size of national economies. An economy producing $500 billion at the beginning of a measuring period and experiencing output growth at 2 per cent a year indicates a larger increment to productive capacity than an economy whose output of $200 billion is expanding at 4 per cent.

Another advantage of an expanding economy, from the viewpoint of military potential, is the relative political ease with which new burdens can be imposed on it. If increased military production is called for, compressing civilian consumption, investment, and nonmilitary public expenditure in a stagnating economy tends to be politically harder than to curb increases in these alternative uses in an expanding economy. It also makes a difference as to whether output expansion results from economic growth or from economic development, if by economic growth we mean output additions produced by the increased employment of labor without improved labor productivity, and if by economic development we mean production increases yielded by increased labor productivity, that is to say, by additions to capital or by improved technology. The difference is that a developing economy, by improving the quality of its resources, tends to raise its capacity for producing technologically more advanced products, a factor with considerable bearing on military potential.

A rapid rate of economic growth and development also indicates the presence of another property that tends to enhance economic potential for producing military strength and for turning to it with dispatch. This is what may be called an economy's resilience or flexibility, which promotes quick adjustment to new tasks of production. A strongly developing economy is characterized by managers and innovators who cultivate the advantages of change, and generally by considerable factor mobility. An expanding economy, moreover, normally has a high rate of savings and investment; and the proportion of resources claimed for this purpose is more easily diverted to the military sector than are the resources claimed for purposes of consumption. The mobility of material wealth is especially great when an already fairly high level of economic development is associated with further expansion.[4]

States differ strikingly in GNP per capita. In 1967, for instance, the United States with $3,985 and Sweden with $3,037 compared with $1,630 in the Soviet Union, $1,158 in Japan, and around an extremely low $100 in China and India.[5] It is often assumed that societies with high increases per capita possess a huge margin of production capacity which can be switched readily to the production of military strength because most consumption is above the level of subsistence and hence can be compressed heavily when the need arises. Some margin of high consumption in affluent societies indeed serves neither natural nor acquired necessities of life, and, being more or less discretionary, is capable of relatively easy compression; and large consumers' inventories, particularly of durable consumers' goods, constitute accumulated "fat," the presence of which decelerates the lowering of consumption levels resulting from postponed replacements. However, these margins of relatively easy compression are far smaller than high-income rates suggest. This is so for two reasons. First, "necessities of life" are defined less by biological needs than by psychological ones, and this makes many consumption habits very insistent. Second, the services characterizing the mechanics of life in rich countries have replaced more primitive (i.e. "cheaper") alternatives. For example, where the private automobile is largely relied upon for getting people to and from their place of work, distances between the places of work and residence have greatly increased, and public means of transportation have withered or are completely absent.

The Structure of Production

Economic military potential is determined by the composition of resources as well as by their over-all magnitude. The production, maintenance, and use of armed forces requires a variety of goods and services. Some of these (e.g. food, clothing, shelter) are of a type which can be produced by economies at a low level of economic and technological development. Technologically more exacting are products (e.g. trucks, gasoline, ships, drugs, radios, guns, and ammunition) which are produced by industrial societies. Most demanding are very complex weapon systems— e.g. nuclear bombs, intercontinental ballistic missiles, modern communications systems, and high-performance aircraft and ships —which are within reach only of countries possessing the most highly developed technology.

As GNP is an index of a country's aggregate resources, so the composition of output reflects the structure of capacity. The composition of the national product is determined by three conditions of supply—manpower, natural resources, and man-made resources (capital and technology)—and by the structure of demand.

The importance of manpower, its size and age composition, is self-evident. In addition to the employed labor force (including manpower in the armed services), each society has a reserve of labor—the unemployed and underemployed, and those not normally seeking employment—which can be tapped in an emergency. The age structure of the population is also relevant. The smaller the proportion of the too young or the too old to work, the greater the state's productive power per million of population.

Rapid population growth, although eventually generating natural additions to the labor force, can be an element of weakness if it greatly increases the cohorts under working age or if, at the other end, it swells the number of those above working age. In 1961, the population of working age (fifteen to sixty-four) varied between 70 and 49 per cent of the population in 128 countries.[6]

The quality of natural resources is obviously crucial to a society's primary industries, agriculture, forestry, and mining. The presence of rich mineral resources, metals, and especially fuel is an obvious asset. Regarding military preparations in time of peace, raw materials can be obtained from foreign resources if local deposits are lacking or are exploitable only at comparatively greater cost. But while self-sufficiency is no advantage in peacetime, it can be in time of war when international commerce can be disrupted by opponents. During the first stages of the industrial revolution, based on coal, iron, and steel, leading military powers were eager to secure sources of supply that were invulnerable to enemy action in time of war. By the beginning of the twentieth century, industrial countries that had come to depend on substantial imports of agricultural products developed an intense concern over their lacking self-sufficiency in food as a weakness in the event of war. In the meantime, however, the importance of natural resources in the military potential of states has suffered a marked decline. On the one hand, by the 1970's the evolution of military technology and the international distribution of military strength greatly reduced expectations of prolonged wars of attrition, as were World Wars I and II. Among the leading military powers, the emphasis was on deterring all-out war between one another, and limited local hostilities were generally assumed to be short or unlikely to interfere dangerously with the flow of indispensable imports. There is one additional reason why natural resources have become less important relative to science and technology as a factor of production and hence as a component of military potential, at least in the highly developed economies. The share in production cost attributable to raw materials declines with the technological sophistication of industrial products. In complex modern weapons, the raw-material content is very low relative to their technological content and their military effectiveness. This permits fewer units to serve the military function previously satisfied by more numerous units of lesser complexity. Moreover, technological progress permits food to be produced with decreasing inputs of land, and allows man-made materials derived from abundant natural resources to be substituted increasingly for scarcer natural materials. In fact many highly industrialized countries, such as Britain and Germany, have a decidedly slender raw-material base; and Japan, without substantial deposits of coal and iron, has nevertheless become the world's third largest producer of steel.

Turning to industrial capacity, a state's military potential tends to be the greater, of course, the larger its normal production of manufactured military supplies. If the armament industry is substantial, there is less need to expand it in the event military demand increases, and it is easier to expand such production, should this become necessary. Regarding other industries, a state's economic potential for generating military strength is the greater, the larger manufacturing is a part of total production; the larger the proportion of durable consumers' goods (e.g. television sets, automobiles) and of capital goods (e.g. machine tools, railroad cars, civilian aircraft, computers) in manufacturing; and the greater the versatility of production managers and workers in shifting to new lines of output. These relationships obtain because the military depend critically on manufactured articles; because durable-goods industries can shift from the production of civilian to that of military hardware (e.g. from civilian to military trucks and to tanks); because capital-goods industries can, in addition, produce the plant and equipment for such conversion; and because managerial and workers' versatility likewise facilitates conversion. To be sure, several service industries—particularly transportation, communication and electric-power productions are no less essential. But the capacity of these industries is associated as a matter of necessity with the industrialization of production.

Indeed, it is these observably close patterns of relationship, based on the fact that the outputs of certain industries are important inputs for other industries, which permits the selection of some single indicators, or a composite of a few indicators, for comparing the military-industrial potential of states. Thus, coal and steel were indubitably key indicators from the middle of the nineteenth century to World Wars I and II. The accompanying tabulation indicates changes in these capacities at that time, and the consequent reshaping of military power.

	COAL PRODUCTION (MILLION TONS)		STEEL PRODUCTION (MILLION TONS)	
	1850	1914	1890	1914
Germany	6.0	277.0	2.3	14.0
France	1.2	40.0	0.7	3.5
Britain	57.0	292.0	3.6	6.5
Russia		36.2	0.4	4.1
United States		455.0	4.3	32.0

SOURCE: Adapted from A. J. P. Taylor, *The Struggle for Mastery in Europe, 1848–1914* (Oxford: Clarendon Press, 1954), Introduction, p. xxx.

While Great Britain was the only important industrial power in 1850, she had been overtaken by 1914. France, the great military power at the beginning of the eighteenth century, was fading in industrial power by its end; and already in 1914, the industrial capacity of the United States rivaled that of Europe taken together. Indeed, in 1913, the United States already possessed 35 per cent of the world's manufacturing capacity.[7]

In the contemporary world, steel output is still fairly representative of industrial power; all the great industrial states are big steel producers. But the production of electric energy has become a better index of the stage of economic and industrial development than the production of coal. The accompanying tabulation shows, for selected countries, the great differences in the national production of steel and electricity.

POWER AND WEALTH

Production of Steel and Electricity, 1969

	CRUDE STEEL (MILLION METRIC TONS)	ELECTRICITY (MILLION KWH)
United States	131.4	1,553
USSR	110.4	689
Japan	81.6	316
West Germany	45.6	226
United Kingdom	26.4	235
India	6.0	49

SOURCE: United Nations, *Monthly Bulletin of Statistics* (March 1971).

While both kinds of production have expanded considerably since 1950 in all these states, expansion has been most dramatic in Japan. In 1964, just five years earlier, she produced only 39.9 million tons of steel and 180 million KWH of electricity.

The element of industrial capacity which is not caught by such indicators is the most advanced technology—for example, electronic communications systems and computers in the 1970's—which leads to very differentiated products, so that output attributable to them is impossible to aggregate nationally and then compare internationally. This obstacle to quantifying and comparing the high technology of national economics is unfortunate, since superior technology has often been a major determinant in the relative military strength of communities. Thus, the introduction of the chariot, the substitution of iron for bronze weapons, the breeding of warhorses, and the inventions of the stirrup, chain mail and the crossbow are examples of military technology that gave a great advantage to the societies introducing them. The long military ascendancy of steppe nomads from central Eurasia was finally and definitively broken by the invention and use of firearms in Europe.

In the modern age, dynamic science and technology are the dominant force in human life. As propellants of continuous change, these key resources affect all branches of production, including management and administration. The demand for technological innovation has engendered the new industry of research and development. Inventions have become far less the product of

single individuals working by themselves than of what may well
be called the modern invention industry. And of particular importance to this new industry has been systematic, science-based
discovery.

Scientific and technological advance boosts military strength
in two ways. First, its discoveries, and innovations based thereon,
benefit military technology directly. Second, there are the indirect benefits of increased labor productivity in the economy,
and hence an increase in economic potential. Technological progress is recognized as the most copious source of increasing labor
productivity; technology is "unquestionably a nation's most important economic resource." [8] Seen statistically, a country's technological capacity consists of its stock of knowledge of how to
produce goods and services, and the diffusion of this know-how
through the labor force by means of education, training, and experience. Seen dynamically, technological excellence reflects the
rate at which this stock of knowledge is enriched.

Since organized Research and Development (R&D) is a crucial determinant of national technological capacity, it would be
illuminating to compare it internationally. Some input data are
available for most countries. Information on R&D expenditures
in the 1960's has the United States far in the lead, spending
nearly ten times as much as the United Kingdom, and indeed
three to four times as much as all European countries (exclusive
of the Communist states) together, 23 times as much as Japan,
and 75 times as much as Italy.[9] (Comparable data for the
Soviet Union are not available.) Data on national manpower
working on R&D also shows the far superior effort made by the
United States. These kinds of information are, however, extremely crude, because prices of research inputs and definitions of
scientific and technological manpower vary substantially from
country to country. The comparative productivity of these factors,
moreover, is impossible to measure.

If one is interested in the economic military potential of states,
the magnitude and productivity of military R&D is of special import. If world expenditures on R&D in general are highly con-

centrated in the industrially advanced countries, this is even more
so with military R&D. Thus, between 1955 and 1965, American
outlays were more than ten times those of Britain and France
together, and the latter two countries accounted for 85 per cent
of all expenditures on military R&D in western Europe. In fact,
at this time, the United States and the Soviet Union are not only
in a class by themselves in this area; they are also the only states
cultivating the frontiers of military technology in all its sections,
and are therefore basically independent of technological inputs
from other states. Even Great Britain and France must import
a considerable proportion of the military technology they consume. The stupendous superiority of the two superpowers in
military R&D is in part a consequence of their rivalry in this
area. Both regard technical excellence and continuous technological innovation as central to their military strength. Neither wants
to fall appreciably behind the other and prefers to move ahead
of it. The arms race between them has therefore centered on
military innovation. In these circumstances, they press military
R&D with far less sensitivity to costs than they do with civilian
R&D.

The recent leadership of the United States in modern technology has engendered appreciable anxiety in Europe over what
Europeans have called the "technology gap," and this has precipitated inquiry into the determinants of rapid technological
growth. While these causes are not as yet well understood, several
plausible hypotheses shed light on the problem.[10] Flourishing
sciences, of course, create the new knowledge on what technological progress feeds. But though excellence in the sciences is a
necessary condition, it is far from sufficient. Among other necessary conditions, there is, first, the practical application of new
knowledge which requires the act of innovation. The innovator is
an entrepreneur, public or private, who invests capital, takes risks,
and provides management for the process of innovation. It is in
this component of an innovating class located in business and
government, whose product in these matters depends upon appropriate motivation as well as skill, which eagerly seeks out and

creates, rather than merely awaits, opportunities for applying new knowledge that recent American superiority is believed to stem from in large part.

Second, technological innovation will tend to flourish in proportion to the funds spent on basic and applied research and on the rewards the innovator receives for achievement. Again, the United States has been excelling in these respects. Third, though the demand for new knowledge and innovation is apt to stimulate an expansion of these activities, over the shorter run, the supply of sufficient inputs is also critical; and this supply has been amply provided in the United States by means of the high and rising proportion of American youth enrolled in higher education and professional training. In 1967, the United States had 436,000 scientists and engineers compared with 148,000 in western Europe.[11] Fourth, several of the most advanced technologies (e.g. nuclear energy, computers) benefit from substantial economies of scale, and the volume of demand generated within a single economy has been much larger in the United States than anywhere else.

Finally, there are complex institutional and cultural conditions which impinge on the national flow of technological innovation. Even though the bulk of R&D funds in the United States, as elsewhere, has come from the public purse, this country has developed a rich variety of institutions—public, private, and semi-public—over which R&D is decentralized, thus encouraging a large number of scientific and technologized initiatives. Furthermore, American society has, so far at least, subjectively thrived under the impetus of variegated and continuous change in the economy. Resistance to the pain of such change seems to be lower, and the drive to push on with technological progress, stronger than in Europe.

Relative technological excellence and its underlying conditions can change rapidly in the modern world. By the early 1970's, Western Europe and Japan were gaining on the United States both as a result of greater efforts in these areas and a lesser one in the United States, where, for instance, federal expenditures on

R&D had been rising sharply and steadily from 1943 to 1967, but fell through 1971 in noninflationary dollars.[12]

The composition of the national output and the structure of productive capabilities behind it are also determined, of course, by the factor of effective demand. Military economic potential is the greater, the more the pattern of demand promotes a supply of productive factors fitting the requirements of military output. This has been a major reason why Soviet governments have persistently favored capital industries as against consumer-goods industries in their economic planning. The most suitable demand, from this point of view, is obviously a large continuous demand for armaments and other military supplies. Technological growth, as we have seen, is stimulated by a strong demand for its fruits. Whether effective demand arises domestically or abroad does not matter. A state exporting a large volume of weapons and military technology enjoys an accordingly larger armaments industry.

Finally, military economic potential is also a consequence of the scale of output, in the aggregate and in particular branches of production. Scale results ultimately from effective demand, which, in turn, is a function of the size of society and its stage of economic development, as far as over-all scale is concerned, and in addition also of the taste of public and private consumers, in the case of particular lines of output.

There are two advantages, the so-called internal and external economies, associated with large scale of production. Internal economies, derived from the expansion of individual enterprises, result mainly from the fact that some productive factors are specialized or indivisible, their use becoming feasible or profitable only when the volume of output is sufficiently large. External economies, derived from the expansion of industry in general, results from a growing supply of labor of various skills, of specialized services and products, etc., on which individual enterprises can draw. National economies that are highly industrialized and of continental size (i.e. the United States and the Soviet Union) afford generous benefits of these kinds; and this is of great importance in the production of advanced military technology. Some objects of military R&D and production are so demanding in their financial and other resource requirements that even industrially advanced states of the size of West Germany or France do not represent a national base large enough to afford a considerable range of projects. For example, this holds true of outer-space exploration, a sophisticated computer industry, or antiballistic missile defense. These types of development and production require huge funds and large combinations of very specialized and expensive manpower and equipment. States of the size and wealth of France or Britain are able to organize on their own a few very big development projects. Even China which, though of huge size, is very underdeveloped economically, has been able to develop nuclear explosives. But these countries are unable to pursue many projects at the same time. They are forced to be selective and hence do not compare with the two superpowers that can afford to tackle a vast range of projects.

International Trade and Finance

By means of foreign trade, states are enabled to specialize on the production of those products, or that over-all output, for which their structure of resources is most suited, or relatively most efficient. The effect is to enhance labor productivity, GNP, and GNP per capita. By improving resource productivity, foreign trade tends thus to increase the military economic potential of states. This follows simply from the principle of comparative advantage elaborated by economists.

There are, however, two considerations pointing to a quali-fication of this conclusion, not as regards the production of in-come and wealth, but concerning the economy as a base of military strength. One of these, which was mentioned in con-nection with the varying endowment of states with natural re-sources, involves the risk inherent in dependence on foreign supplies of raw materials, semimanufactures, and manufactured products essential to the production of national military capabilities. The risk is that the inflow of foreign supplies may be reduced or stopped by the action of other states. The extent of the risk depends on the criticality of foreign supplies to military production and on the degree to which the advance stockpiling of reserve supplies and the emergency rationing of reduced supplies or domestic substitutes are unlikely to permit essential requirements to be met in an emergency. The importance of the risk to the policy-maker depends on the perceived likelihood of contingencies in which the risk would materialize and prove crippling. Dependence on foreign trade for vital imports, which is economically efficient, is tolerable if a state depends on several foreign sources of supply, and if its government sees little danger of this trade being disrupted seriously. Nevertheless, this risk has induced many states in the past to maintain, and protect from foreign competition, domestic production, even though the price of doing so was paid in terms of lowered productivity in the national economy.

As a basis of national military strength, unrestricted foreign trade would yield maximum benefits when a state possesses comparative advantage precisely in those industries which are essential to the production of military strength. Great Britain enjoyed this advantage to a very substantial extent during the middle third of the nineteenth century, when large exports greatly expanded the capacity of her capital-goods and other manufacturing industries. She lost this advantage gradually as the industrial newcomers—especially Germany, France, and the United States—cut into her industrial lead. To a degree, this advantage occurs today to all countries exporting a substantial volume of capital goods and of goods embodying advanced technology.

The second consideration, which is a special case of the first, concerns the importation of arms. Again, in strictly economic terms, this may be the cheapest way of acquiring armaments. In fact, most countries are at present unable to produce all modern weapons they require, so that their freedom of choice is limited to the question of relying on foreign producers more or less, a varying proportion of imports being a necessity. There are several drawbacks attached, in the eyes of many governments and societies, to dependence on foreign arms. First, such dependence may be sensed to conflict with national pride and prestige. Second, there is again the risk that imports may be cut off in time of war. Third, the choice of foreign suppliers may raise questions of political constraint. Alliance relationships may preclude shopping for the best bargain; or the exporting state may exact some political *quid pro quo,* formally or informally, a situation not unlikely to arise when the importing country needs credits. Indeed, once there is considerable dependence on foreign arms supplies from a particular exporting country, the importing state is not seldom at the mercy of the supplier. Thus, following the Kashmir war between India and Pakistan in 1965, the United States, a major arms supplier to both, suspended shipments for a time. After the Israeli-Arab war of 1967, France declared an arms embargo against Israel, which had its air force equipped with French jet fighters; and in 1970–1971, the United States exploited Israeli dependence on American weapons in order to press Israel for concessions paving the way to a peace settlement with the Arab states. The export of nuclear weapons, moreover, has been prevented, at first by the unilateral policy of nuclear-weapons states and, since 1970, by the adoption of the international Non-Proliferation Treaty. It is not surprising, in view of these disadvantages of dependence on foreign weapons, that many states regard it as a serious source of weakness and will turn to domestic production if this is a feasible option, even though expensive.

On the other hand, large exports of arms bolster the economic military potential. The United States, the Soviet Union, France, and Great Britain have been the chief exporting countries during the 1950's and 1960's.[13] In these cases, unless they constitute re-export of arms previously imported, foreign demand brings into existence additional production facilities that may be regarded as reserve capacity for national use in an emergency.

International finance also impinges on the military economic potential of states. The ability of a country to run a substantial import surplus—on the strength of large holdings of foreign currencies and gold or on the strength of borrowing power—permits it, for a time at least, to increase the build-up of military strength accordingly. Foreign investments are an asset from this point of view. During World War II, Britain sold $4.2 billion of her external investments and was thereby enabled to make a greater war effort than she could have otherwise. In the late 1960's, the United States experienced a sharply rising deficit in its balance of payments and was able to find external finance for the war in Vietnam in large part only because the Japanese and several west European governments accumulated vast holdings of dollars. To the extent of the import surplus, a state draws on the productive capacity of other states either by importing arms or materials and other products needed for armaments production, or indirectly by either importing civilian supplies or exporting less in order to release more productive resources to producing military capabilities. *Economic* potential is not involved, of course, if a state is enabled to manage an import surplus as a result of gifts or credits extended for *political* reasons. Even though such benefits are wed to political considerations, they will nevertheless increase economic military potential to the extent of the loan or gift.

The balance-of-payments position and reserves of international liquidity (gold and foreign exchange) of a state affect also the foreign deployment and use of military forces. The fleets that the United States and the Soviet Union maintain far from their own shores cause foreign-exchange outlays and so do troops and bases maintained abroad (except to the extent that allies are willing to bear all or some of the costs contracted in local currency). The large-scale intervention of the United States in Vietnam occasions sizable outlays of foreign exchange for supporting goods and services purchased abroad. Therefore, a strong position of international liquidity is an asset which is part of the military potential of great powers interested in using military strength in distant lands and oceans. To be sure, if large increases in foreign-exchange expenditures become necessary as a result of foreign-policy decisions, a state can, of course, attempt to curtail other types of external outlays, i.e. merchandise imports, tourist expenditure, foreign economic aid, and foreign investment. But, except in an emergency, these expenditures are not easily cut because they are important to individuals, firms, and government departments. From this point of view, for example, the American ability to play the role of a world power was gradually diminished by persistent weakness in the balance of payments by the United States during the 1960's.

The significance of military economic potential varies with the type of military conflict or effort with which governments are concerned. This becomes clear at once if one distinguishes between nuclear deterrence, conventional war, and guerrilla activities. These types of military confrontation make vastly different technological demands, even though high-level technological capabilities can be applied effectively for any type. The significance of national military potential also varies with the capabilities of likely military opponents. A state with a modest potential can be a match for others in its class or by dint of a high degree of mobilization, even for a state superior in economic potential. Finally, the significance of potential varies with the foreign-policy posture of states. If countries do not entertain objectives calling for the aggressive employment of military power against other countries, if they seek to avoid serious intrastate conflicts, or if they can count on military backing by other states, their requirements for military strength will be correspondingly low. But in a world in which contingencies are hard to foresee, and in which collective security has received only rudimentary development, the demand for military strength will seldom be negligible, only ceremonial or zero.

The question is often raised whether differences between capitalist and socialist economic systems entail differences in military economic potential. While there can be no definitive answer to this question, it is suggested that this association is weak and overshadowed by differences in other conditions. To begin with, differences between economic systems are often associated with differences between political systems, and these may influence a state's political and administrative capacity for generating military strength. For instance, if a state has a Soviet-type economy *and* strong authoritarian leadership, its government is in a political position to impose a high rate of savings and investment. If the type of economic system affects *economic* military potential, it must do so by influencing the rate of economic, industrial, and technological progress, the degree to which the industrial structure facilitates military production, and, possibly, the external financial standing of the country. It is, however, impossible to identify such effects and isolate them from the impingement of other factors which influence these phenomena.

First, pure economic systems are not encountered in the real world, all actual systems being varying mixtures of pure types. The difference between the Soviet and American systems is appreciably smaller than that between pure command and pure market economy or between pure socialist and pure capitalist systems. The economic order of societies in the same category also exhibits a great deal of variation. As the French, Japanese, Italian, and American systems differ, so do those of the Soviet Union, China, Poland, and Yugoslavia. Second, differences in national economic performance result in considerable part from differing physical resources, in cultural standards that impinge on work performance, and in the factor of size and scale. Third and foremost, differences in economic capability are determined crucially by the relative stage of economic development.

Administrative Skill

In order to comprehend fully the bearing of economic on military strength, it is necessary to recognize the impact of the two other foundations of national military power and the relationship between all three bases. These other foundations are the political determination to produce and use military strength, and the skills involved in fashioning military strength from the inputs made available by society. Political determination causes a proportion of national manpower and other resources to be allotted to the military sector. These resources must be transformed into suitable military capabilities, and this transformation can be effected with more or less skill. The greater this skill, the more military strength will be derived from allocated resources. Or, to put it differently, the magnitude of inputs required for producing a desired level and kind of military strength depends on the efficiency of the transformation process. It is this matter of administrative competence—a component of national military potential to which we will turn first.[14] Those skills of labor and management which are part of the national economy and determine the productivity of labor are part of, and have been discussed as part of, *economic* potential. The crucial elements of skill that remain to be noted are those in the armed services and in the parts of civilian government concerned with the generation of military strength. These sets of officials are not passive recipients of resources diverted to foreign and military policy.

In the modern era, administrative skill is involved in making numerous interlocking decisions on what sort of military capabilities to produce from given resources: definition of the contingencies to be prepared for in the light of the military forces of other powers; the over-all force structure; the distribution of military manpower over different types of forces, e.g. air force, navy, army; the most efficient combinations of men, training, and machines; the composition of weaponry; the size and composition of military stocks; the recruitment, education, and training of officers and men; and the method of financing military spending. These and many other problems, each composed of numerous subproblems, must be solved in a co-ordinated manner; and how well this task is performed greatly affects the positive military power that states generate.

Various bureaucratic bodies in the civilian and military structure of government are involved in designing the military output, and in implementing the design. The administrative performance is, of course, subject to the classical problems of *all* bureaucratic administration, for example, of how to decentralize administrative efforts without loss of central direction. But there are also administrative problems peculiar to military planning.

The central administrative problem is to define the missions to be prepared for and to select the cheapest set of alternative means toward performing them effectively. The operative criteria are the needs to meet the capabilities of potential adversaries and to economize resources. Satisfying these criteria is extremely difficult in a complex, dynamic environment with reference to *future* contingencies which have necessarily uncertain identity and properties. And this fundamental difficulty in military planning has been magnified in recent decades by the rapidity of change in the relevant environments, including the technological environment. Accelerating inventions and innovations in military technology have led to an alarming rate of obsolescence of armaments and forces, thus giving military R&D a role of crucial importance, making the specification of options very risky, and rendering choices extremely expensive.

The second criterion poses no less a problem. Even the wealthiest countries are beset by limits, economic and political, to what they can afford in the military sector. The imperative necessity to economize, therefore, produces endless choices directed toward achieving maximum military worth from a given volume of inputs.

Scientific and technological progress benefit the element of *expertise* in meeting the two criteria, and increased expertise reduces reliance on sheer judgment and can make judgment more informed. This benefit accrues not only as far as apparatus is concerned (e.g. modern communications and computer systems), but also in the form of newly developed techniques of analysis, such as econometric forecasting, cost-effectiveness studies, and the tool of planning-programming-budgeting (PPB). The introduction of such techniques and instruments amounts to a major management revolution.[15] However, none of these innovations in management solve the administrative problems automatically. Their application cannot do without crucial inputs of judgment. The derivation of efficient devices therefore requires a skill which is in the nature of an art rather than a science. And this requirement is made more exacting because the process of turning resources into ready military strength is not only a technical problem, it is also a *political* problem. Different government and military leaders, bureaucratic departments, and outside interest-groups see administrative choices partly in terms of how their own political, professional, and pecuniary interests are affected by the outcome. Indeed, the technical limitations of policy analysis naturally permit self-interest and politics to intrude. When information is soft, prediction controversial, and conclusions noncompelling, people can choose to reject analyses and conclusions whose implications run counter to the interests they embody or represent.

The Political Component

Having defined economic and administrative capacity as bases of national military strength, we must now turn to the remaining basis or bases. What else is there?

Historians have noted a variety of conditions that appeared to them to explain the military strength of societies through the ages. Sometimes they emphasize one factor, sometimes a combination of factors. Invariably, they point to the importance of political, social, and cultural factors. History indeed suggests that the military potential of societies rests in substantial part on political and cultural factors. If these discourage the production and maintenance of military strength, economic and administration capabilities will not come into play for this purpose. As actualization of putative power depends crucially on the will, manifest or presumed, to use force, so economic and administrative resources do not generate putative power without the *will* to build national strength.

Military strength does not come about unless a society, acting through effective authorities, determines the proportion of manpower and other resources to be allocated to the military sector. It is for this reason that changes in defense budgets receive considerable attention. However, even though such changes express a shift in national preferences, they are too aggregative for our purpose; they reflect things between which it is useful to make distinctions, namely between the determinants of potential military power and those factors which determine the mobilization of this potential; that is, *antecedent* conditions must be separated from *situational* conditions.

The degree to which a state mobilizes potential depends obviously upon the international situation, the challenges and opportunities it presents, and relevant means-ends calculations, as perceived by government, other leaders, and that part of the public which takes an interest in foreign affairs and has some influence to bring their views to bear. A community may be more or less divided in these terms, and this lack of unity will affect the degree of mobilization that can be achieved. But the response thus provoked by the external stimulus is conditioned by antecedent factors that predispose a society toward a military reaction, or facilitate this result. These factors constitute the political and cultural component in the military potential of states.

There are four such antecedent factors.[16] First, there is the population's underlying propensity to mobilize and use military strength internationally. This attitude complex, which favors more or less a military response to international situations of conflict, is what historians have in mind when they characterize communities as more or less warlike or militaristic. It is a settled sensitivity to the advantages and disadvantages of employing force internationally. The greater the sensitivity to the advantages, and the less the sensitivity to the cost (material, moral, etc.) of resorting to military force offensively or defensively, the more "warlike" is the society concerned. Whatever the pattern is, it is part of the political culture transmitted from one generation to another, but subject to the relevant impacts, reinforcing or disillusioning, of historical experience.

The second factor in the political basis for military power is the predisposition, which can be low or high, to support the community. This attitude is rooted in a sense of solidarity which ties citizens to state-organized society. It is also a part of political culture. It is not specifically sensitive to military matters, but tends to come into play when a national emergency has been precipitated. If the emergency is military, this disposition favors behavior toward a "closing of ranks" in the face of danger and toward suspending ordinary political partisanship.

The third factor is the public disposition to support the foreign and military policy of the government, or to accept it as authoritative and hence binding, simply because these matters of policy are regarded as belonging properly to the initiative of the authorities. Finally, support for the government's production and use of military strength tends to accrue from groups that have a direct and specific interest in these activities, that is to say, from people who expect to derive personal advantages as a result. Thus, this usually holds true of a considerable proportion of the military who may benefit in terms of career interests, professional relevance, and social prestige. It may also hold true of business interests which derive profit from the production of armaments and military supplies. And national military enterprise may supply psychological income to people who welcome participation in it as an exciting release from a humdrum routine life or as a satisfaction of other personal needs originating in personality structure.

By the end of the 1960's, there was increasing evidence that the political, but not the economic and administrative, basis of national military strength had become seriously eroded in the affluent societies of the West. In most of these countries, pressure on defense budgets indicated that the opportunity costs of military preparedness had risen sharply. The modern "consumers' society" was preoccupied with enjoying a rapidly rising level of income and leisure and with diverting public expenditures toward the alleviation of environmental deterioration brought about by rapid and carefree industrialization. Aversion to war, precipitated by the experience of destructive wars, and reinforced by the awesome specter of nuclear disaster, and the dissipation of the traditional military ethic combined to make military service increasingly repugnant to youth.[17] Identification with state, government, and elites declined as loyalties became more fluid and diffuse, and the consent of the governed more contractual, to be continuously renegotiated on a *quid-pro-quo* basis.

Are differences in political systems regularly associated with political potential for generating and using political strength? De Tocqueville, for instance, attributed a strong potential of this kind to aristocratic and a low potential to democratic countries.[18] Or it may be held that leaders in authoritarian regimes do not require public support but can simply command acceptance of their decisions and are, furthermore, in a position to mold public opinion and attitudes. The historical record, however, shows militarily weak authoritarian and strong democratic countries as well as these expected results. The Ottoman empire during the nineteenth century and Russia from 1900 to 1917 were remarkably weak, and numerous defections of Soviet citizens in the early phases of World War II disclosed that the Stalin government had only a precarious hold over the public. Britain did extremely well in World War II, and so did democratic Finland in 1938–1939 in its war against the Soviet Union.

If differences in political regime *per se* impinge on military potential, we do not have enough cases of adequate comparability to establish them statistically. On the basis of our limited knowledge in this respect, it is probable that such associations are not strong, that is to say, that their effects, if any, are overshadowed by other differences. This becomes plausible if one looks at the particular sources of political potential we have identified. First, the predisposition to support the use of military strength is an element of political culture which has appeared to be strong in recent decades in countries with such disparate political systems as Japan, Germany, Great Britain, Finland, the Soviet

Union, both Koreas, Israel, and the United States. Second, the degree of national solidarity originates in political integration and is inhibited where various kinds of cleavages are sharply felt. Authoritarian regimes do not appear to be either disadvantaged or advantaged in this respect compared with democratic societies (although adverse fissures in authoritarian societies may be less visible before critical tests occur). Third, the disposition to accept government decisions on matters of foreign and military policy automatically seems to vary a great deal, irrespective of type of regime, and probably depends on government performance in terms of collective preferences as well as on culture. Finally, interest groups desiring direct benefit from the military build-ups can presumably exist under any form of government. As was observed with reference to the impact of *economic* systems, it may be hypothesized that the impact of *political* systems also is dominated by the consequences flowing from different stages of development.

Some Conclusions

Having identified the constituents of the military potential of states, it remains to relate them briefly to one another and to the international conflict situations in which they become significant. When states are engaged in war, their unmobilized potential becomes a factor in government decisions on continuing, escalating or terminating the conflict. When a state uses the threat of force, and the leaders of the threatened country speculate about the merits of defense, they will consider not only the ready military capabilities of the threatening state, but also its ability to mobilize additional strength. And to the extent that states forego certain actions when unthreatened in order to avoid a confrontation with a militarily superior country, the latter's military potential, particularly its political disposition to resort to force, is a crucial factor.

Within some range, superior endowment with one base of military strength can compensate for lesser assets in another base. For example, State A may equal B's military strength, even though appreciably inferior in economic resources (resulting from smaller size or lesser development), because it musters the determination to allocate a larger share of its resources to producing military strength, and/or excels in relevant administrative competence. The ability of the Peoples' Republic of China to develop nuclear armament is a case in point. Societies excelling in economic wealth may nevertheless grudge the allocation of sizable resources to the military sector. They can also afford a low level of administrative efficiency in turning so allocated resources into military capabilities. Indeed, as with organizations generally, the ability to afford slack often begets the practice, whereas efficiency is more urgently in demand in a taut system.[19]

The significance of various components of military potential depends naturally on the kind of interstate situations in which a state's military strength is an essential factor; and governments may entertain more or less correct assumptions about the properties of such contingencies. Deploying nuclear forces for deterrence, preparing for conventional war for defense of the territory, or in distant theaters, or for fighting guerrillas abroad, clearly make different demands on a country's military potential. Thus, employing conventional forces for coercive threats calls for different skills and for a different political propensity to resort to force than defending the home territory against conventional attack. Military intervention in foreign civil wars calls for different skills and military capabilities than participation in a naval armaments race. Geographic location has a bearing on the need for military potential; New Zealand, for instance, is in a quite different position than Israel or Thailand. The political and cultural bases for generating and using military power are apt to show considerable differentiation. For instance, a particular society may have a strong determination to defend itself against attack while lacking any disposition to become a military aggressor. Switzerland has shown this attitude over the past hundred years. Or a society may have a high political readiness to engage in war against certain states (for historical, ideological, or other reasons) but not against others. Thus, though states have general bases for producing and applying military strength, the suitability of their national potential varies with different exigencies of particular conflict situations.

Notes

1. The following discussion of economic strength as a component of the military potential of societies is a condensation of the more detailed treatment in Klaus Knorr, *Military Power and Potential* (Lexington, Mass.: Heath, 1970), chap. III.

2. This figure and the following are taken from: United States Arms Control and Disarmament Agency, *World Military Expenditures* (Washington: 1969).

3. For an analysis of these difficulties, see any good textbook on economics. It is worth noting that the calculation of Soviet military expenditure is specially difficult. According to Soviet data published at the 24th Congress of the Soviet Communist Party, military expenditures averaged 7 per cent of GNP from 1966 to 1970. However, a major part of expenditures on science, averaging 3 per cent, must be added. *New York Times,* (April 8, 1971), p. 1.

4. R. H. Hawtrey, *Economic Aspects of Sovereignty* (London: Longmans, Green, 1930), pp. 84–92.

5. U.S. Arms Control and Disarmament Agency, *World Military Expenditures* (1969), p. 20.

6. Bruce M. Russell, *et al., World Handbook of Political and Social Indicators* (New Haven: Yale University Press, 1964), pp. 25–27.

7. *Ibid.,* p. xxxi.

8. Jacob Schmookler, *Innovation and Economic Growth* (Cambridge, Mass.: Harvard University Press, 1966), p. 2.

9. For a collection of data, see Knorr, *Military Power and Potential,* pp. 76–80.

10. For a more detailed discussion, see *ibid.,* pp. 83–90.

11. Cf. Jean-Jacques Salomon, "Europe and the Technology Gaps," *International Studies Quarterly,* 15 (1971): 11–13.

12. *The New York Times* (Oct. 31, 1971), p. 62.

13. John L. Sutton and Geoffrey Kemp, *Arms to Developing Countries, 1945–1965* (London: *Adelphi Papers,* No. 28, 1966).

14. For a more detailed discussion of these administrative capabilities, see Knorr, *Military Power and Potential,* chap. IV.

15. Cf. Alain C. Enthoven and K. Wayne Smith, *How Much Is Enough: Shaping the Defense Program, 1961–1969* (New York: Harper & Row, 1971).

16. For a more detailed discussion, see Knorr, *Military Power and Potential,* chap. V.

17. Cf. Christoph Bertram, "Internal Pressures behind Defence Policies in Western Europe," *Survival,* 13 (Jan. 1971): 13–16.

18. Alexis de Tocqueville, *Democracy in America,* 2 vols. (New York: Knopf, 1960), I: 228 and 234; II: 264.

19. Albert O. Hirschman, *Exit, Voice and Loyalty* (Cambridge, Mass.: Harvard University Press, 1970), pp. 6–13.

CHAPTER

4

The Bases of National Economic Power

Economic wealth is convertible into virtually all types of power and influence. As we have seen in Chapter 3, it is a basis of military power. It figures as one foundation of international prestige. In the conduct of international propaganda, foreign intelligence, and bribery, it is an indispensable subsidiary to skill. It is also a basis of national economic power, which is the subject of the present chapter. What exactly is national economic power? How does it become effective? Which are its bases? How can these bases be promoted? What are the costs of, and hence resistances to, their promotion? How do big and little, and rich and poor, states differ in the bases of economic power? Do national economic systems affect the economic power of states? Logically, we must begin with defining national economic power —a subject which has received far less analytical attention than national military power—and with identifying the types of uses to which it gives rise, and then deduce the foundation on which it rests.

There are two sides to national economic power. One, the active side, is concerned with what a country can do to other countries; the other, passive side, concerns a country's ability to limit what other countries do to it. From the first point of view, national economic power is the ability of a state to benefit itself, using economic or financial policy, by hurting, or threatening to hurt, benefiting, or promising to benefit, weakening or strengthening another state economically. From the second viewpoint, national economic power is a state's ability to limit such use of economic power by other states against itself. In the following, unless otherwise specified, the term "economic power" refers to its active, outwardreaching form.

The benefits a state derives, or its government intends to derive, from employing economic power can be political and military as well as economic. Thus, A may obtain diplomatic support on certain international issues, or a military ally regarding actual or potential conflicts, by offering to buy more of B's goods, or to sell B more of scarce goods, or to extend loans or gifts to B. A may threaten B with equivalent disadvantages, should the latter cease to give diplomatic support or to remain an ally. A may want to damage B, who is an actual or potential opponent by acts designed to reduce the latter's economic or political basis for military or economic power. Or A may want to strengthen B, who is a diplomatic supporter or military ally, by acts designed to improve the latter's base of military and economic power.

Certain phenomena are excluded from the present consideration of national economic power. First, the following analysis will disregard the use of market power (i.e. a monopolist or monopsonist position), not to weaken or coerce other states, but simply in order to secure income gains resulting from an improvement in the terms of trade (i.e. the price ratio of exports relative to imports) in regular markets for goods and services. Such exploitation of international market power is not unimportant; and it receives analysis in theories of international trade. We disregard the phenomenon here only because it lacks interest from the viewpoint of Chapters 6 to 7. We will simply assume that, when acting rationally, governments tend to exploit international market power for economic gains as a matter of course, unless, or to the extent not, restrained by the following reasons: (a)

ignorance of the existence of market power; (b) market uncertainties which make it difficult to design a trade policy calculated to improve the terms of trade; (c) retaliation by other
states is likely to reduce or preclude net gains; (d) short-term
gains are liable to be offset by long-term disadvantages (e.g.
external reactions will gradually reduce market power); (e)
undesirable side effects, for example of a political character, out-
weigh income gains; and (f) there is a countervailing interest in
benefiting another country or countries. However, if A manipu-
lates the terms of trade for the purpose of hurting, threatening,
or weakening other states, then there is an exercise of economic
power within the area of our interest. Second, there are other uses
of economic policy which, though suited as a means to affect
other countries deliberately, may be adopted exclusively in order
to satisfy a domestic interest. Thus, protective import tariffs may
be introduced for the purpose of benefiting the interest of politically influential domestic producers, or for shaping national
production capacity in the interest of economic military potential,
or for curtailing domestic unemployment. Any effects of policy
on other states are purely incidental. These essentially inward-
directed policies are studied in books on international trade theory
and policy.

Third, we will also exclude from the subject of national economic
power a part of what François Perroux calls economic domination
or dominance.[1] According to Perroux, as the real world is one
of unequal business firms, so it is one of unequal national economies, some dominant and some dominated. A dominant economy
is one which, because of its large size (in terms of GNP, advanced
stage of development, and large share in international economic
transactions), will affect other national economies of lesser size
and development more than it is affected by them. Its foreign trade
and financial transactions, though figuring importantly in the
economies of other countries, are less important to itself in relation
to GNP. In other words, dominance exists when economic events
and domestic economic policies in A persistently affect economic

events and policies in B more than the other way round. Thus, Perroux regards the present American economy as the world-dominating economy of first rank. Any changes in a dominating economy in price levels and structure, in the rate of employment, investment, and economic growth, and in output composition, radiate out to, and strongly impinge on, lesser economies, the impact being the greater, the more important foreign economic and financial transactions are to them. In order to clarify the consequences of this condition, we will distinguish economic dominance from economic domination. Both relationships are characterized by unequal economic constraints. If the constraint is produced involuntarily, it indicates economic dominance; if it is deliberate, it indicates economic domination. Beyond doubt, the massive weight of the American economy in the world gives it dominance. But most events in the American economy, whether planned or unplanned, take place without any intent to impose their repercussions on other economies. Such effects are incidental. Similarly, economic dominance may reflect superior economic innovation that is not cultivated, at least primarily, to cause adjustments in other economies. Countries do not contract economic depression or inflation, and governments do not ordinarily foster economic growth in order to benefit or hurt other countries.

Next, strictly commercial or quasi-commercial exchanges do not involve economic power so long as benevolence or malevolence is absent from the conduct of the public actors. For example, no use of power takes place when two state-trading states negotiate an exchange of exports without any insertion of threats or blandishments designed to affect the behavior of the other side. Although the actors are governments, the transaction is then equivalent to a commercial contract between private firms. The United States repeatedly bought territory from other sovereign states. The United States bought the Louisiana territory from France in 1803, for $12 million, and Florida from Spain in 1819 for $5 million; and the Virgin Islands were bought from Denmark in 1917. These were not examples *per se* of economic power.

To put it differently, national economic wealth is not the same as national economic power. Wealth, to be sure, is an asset useful internationally for a vast range of pure exchanges; and wealth is also a basis of economic power. National economic power is involved when wealth or economic policy is used *deliberately* to modify the behavior or capabilities of other states. This matter of intent is crucial to the exercise of power. There may be bargaining, but there is no politics in a purely commercial exchange. There is politics in the exercise of economic power.

In order to elucidate the foregoing definition of national economic power, both the power consequences and the power instruments require more elaborate descriptions. As elaborated in Chapter 1, the distinct purposes of applying national *military* power (putative) are, first, to threaten injury to an opponent or to continue hurting him if force is already in use; and second, to take or defend some contested objective of value by sheer force. These purposes may also be pursued indirectly by giving military support to another country.

National *economic* power can be used in precisely the same ways. First, it may be employed coercively, i.e., to hurt another country economically, or to continue hurtful sanctions already in force. Or the promise of economic reward may be held out in attempting to influence a foreign government's behavior. Second, economic power can be applied to damaging or weakening another country without coercive attempt to make another actor do something he would not otherwise do. Four subcategories of this use can be distinguished: (1) causing another country to lose income, employment, investment and economic growth, or inducing or reinforcing inflationary or balance-of-payments pressure, in order to generate political discontent and disunity; (2) reducing another country's military economic potential either by producing general effects as discussed under (1), or by minimizing the development of capabilities specific to military production (e.g. armaments industries or industries especially supportive of armaments production); (3) interfering with an ongoing military mobilization or war effort by measures causing general effects as discussed under (1), or by curtailing the import of essential inputs (e.g. raw materials or fuel) and thus causing bottlenecks in production; and (4) reducing another state's economic power by the generally weakening measures discussed under (1) or by reducing specific sources of economic strength (e.g. monopolist or monopsonist positions). Third, and conversely, various economic measures can be used to strengthen another state (1) by promoting its income, increasing its rates of employment, investment, and growth, or helping it to damp down inflation or to relieve balance-of-payments pressures; (2) by promoting its economic base for military strength; (3) by assisting its effort of military mobilization or war; and (4) by bolstering its national economic power. Fourth, national economic power can be used by a state also for strengthening its own foundations as specified below. The object in this case is to increase the state's putative economic power. Occasionally, and finally, like any other form of power, national economic power can be used to inflict punishment, not for purposes of coercion, but for strictly emotional satisfaction.

The instruments through which states can exercise economic power for the purposes set forth are extremely variegated.[2] They may be used either to impinge on particular commodity markets, enterprises, and industries or to influence macroeconomic conditions, e.g. GNP, economic development, or general price level, in the other state. These instruments obviously involve foreign commercial investment and aid and foreign-exchange policies; but they include also many domestic policies, e.g. fiscal, monetary, taxation, and immigration. In the following, only the principal instruments will be considered:

1.   a. *A* reduces imports from *B* by means of an embargo, import duties, or quotas, foreign-exchange control, or other restrictive measures, including the closing or restriction of transit facilities. *A* reduces *B*'s exports to third countries by subsidizing and dumping its own competitive exports, by concluding long-term trade agreements with third countries, by putting pressures on third states to restrict imports from *B*, etc.
     b. *A* acts to increase *B*'s exports by the opposite measures of those mentioned under (a).

2. a. *A* acts to reduce *B*'s imports by an export embargo or other export restrictions, by refusing or curtailing credits and other aid to *B*, by prevailing on third states to act in a similar restrictive fashion, and under exceptional circumstances (e.g. in time of war) by restricting transit and by blacklisting exporters to *B* in third countries.

b. *A* acts to increase *B*'s imports by using the same policy for reverse effect.

3. a. *A* benefits employment, investment, and economic development in *B* by means of public loans or gifts, promoting direct private investment in *B*, and by extending technical assistance.

b. *A* acts to reduce employment, investment, and development in *B* by the opposite measures.

Of diverse other ways of exercising economic power, the following seem worth mentioning:

4. a. *A* acts to put *B*'s international currency position under pressure by selling holdings of *B*'s currency, inducing short-term capital movements from *B,* or by other techniques.

b. *A* acts to relieve pressure on *B*'s international payments position by reverse measures of the kind mentioned under (a).

5. *A* harms *B* by running up trade deficits, repudiating or suspending service on debts owed to *B*, and confiscating, freezing, or putting various adverse pressures on enterprises *B* owns in *A*.

6. *A* penetrates *B*'s economy by means of direct investments, cartel arrangements, and technical assistance, even by bribery sometimes, and uses positions of influence thus acquired in order to harm or benefit *B*.

As even this summary list reveals, some policy instruments can be used for achieving various effects, and the same effect can be achieved by several policy instruments applied singly or jointly.

Having concluded that national economic power encompasses the ability of a state to employ these measures and achieve the stated effects, we can now inquire into the bases of this ability or, more generally, of the putative economic power of states. Obviously, as army divisions *per se* are not military power, so GNP or national wealth *per se* is not economic power. The phenomenon is more complex. The putative economic power of states has four bases: "economic strength"; the will to use this strength for power purposes; the skill of applying this strength for such purposes; and the international reputation a state has in terms of an expected disposition to use its economic strength in order to exercise power.

Economic Strength

The sheer magnitude of a state's foreign economic transactions is one element of national economic strength. Obviously, a country accounting for thirty per cent of world exports and imports and of world exports of capital and technical assistance, tends to enjoy far greater leverage than a country accounting for only three per cent. However, it is not advantageous from this point of view that the state's trade and capital exports are also large in relation to GNP. If its trade is large in these terms as well, the country is also susceptible to economic pressure from the outside. In other words, while it provides leverage for application to other states, an important constituent of active economic power, a large volume of trade relative to GNP also tends to reduce passive economic power. Moreover, the larger trade is in relation to GNP, the more difficult will power-induced changes in exports and imports tend to be because of domestic economic disturbances experienced at home. From this point of view then, the United States is superior to the United Kingdom not only because American trade is larger, but also because American trade is much smaller than Britain's in relation to GNP.

Size of foreign trade varies mainly with size of population, degree of economic development, and the degree of international economic specialization. The implications of population size and stage of development are obvious. Even though India is a poor country, it has a larger foreign trade than Switzerland, which is rich; but Switzerland's foreign trade per capita is a multiple of India's. Clearly also, a country's foreign trade will tend to vary with the extent to which it is engaged in the international division of labor. This variable, in turn, is principally the consequence of trade policy (e.g. free trade versus protectionism), of breadth of endowment with natural and other resources, and of size of territory (i.e. internal transportation costs, like international transport costs, act like an equivalent import duty). A country's ability to acquire leverage from capital export is also in part a consequence of size (i.e. GNP, which reflects size of population and degree of economic development). If we assume funds for export to come from savings and taxes, or more generally speaking from economic surplus above private and public consumption and capital maintenance, the size of these funds, given the rate of savings and taxation, depends on the size of GNP.

Economic power, however, is a matter of structure as well as magnitude. Economic strength as a basis of national economic power is not the same as economic wealth, although wealth is an ingredient of it. Similarly, economic strength is not simply measured by the volume of a country's trade, even though such trade is another variable condition from which strength is derived. In order to serve the purposes of economic power, a country's economic capabilities and economy must have certain structural characteristics just as such a special (but different) economic structure is needed for the production of military strength. If we concentrate on the ability to alter international merchandise, service, and capital flows, a state would be equipped *structurally* with an ideal base for exercising economic power, if (1) it exported things in urgent demand abroad while importing things regarding which its own demand was highly elastic, and if (2) it held monopoly control over the supply of things demanded by foreign importing countries and monopsony control over the goods foreign countries have to export. Structural conditions also impinge on the ability of states to export capital. Whatever the size of GNP, the propensity to restrain consumption, public or private, is an important factor. In other words, national economic strength will tend to be the greater, the less the outside world can do without its exports and without its domestic market.

There are, of course, no states in the real world fully ideally meeting these structural descriptions. For a few years following World War II, the United States came closer to the ideal base than any other country has ever achieved. But this resulted from evidently exceptional circumstances. The bulk of the world was then impoverished and economically disorganized. To generalize with reference to the real world, the more a state's international economic position approximates the ideal construct, the stronger it will tend to be in terms of economic power. Conversely, the less it approximates the specified characteristics, the weaker a state will tend to be in these terms.

Since presumably no state is interested in exercising economic power vis-à-vis the entire outside world all at once, but rather vis-à-vis a particular state or group of states, the structural desiderata are not as exacting as the ideal type suggests. Even potential economic power depends then on particular actor relationships of conceivable interest. This is so also in the case of potential military power. There is, however, an important difference between the exercise of economic and military power. In the event of a military conflict between A and B, the number of other states supporting A or B is not usually large. Participation tends to be costly. In the event of a purely economic conflict, however, it is usually in the interest of most other states to provide the opponents with alternative markets and sources of supply. For instance, if A places an embargo on B's exports, B will attempt to shift its exports to other markets. This would impose some difficulties of adjustment but no further ill effects if A, needing the type of goods it had imported from B, switches its purchases to other sources of supply. On the other hand, B's position would be weaker, and A's stronger, if B had an important high-cost export industry for which A had been the sole or principal outlet. In that case, A's embargo would compel B either to export subsidized goods, or to suffer unemployment in its export industry, likewise with an income-depressing effect and with the consequent burden of shifting resources to other fields of production. This example, which can be paralleled by one involving A's resort to an embargo of its own exports to B, points up the importance of structural factors and size of market. A holds a degree of economic power over B only if A's trade is worth something to B, in that it is important in scale and irreplaceable, or hard to replace, and if B is more dependent economically on A than the other way round.

International currency reserves and gold are of some significance to national economic power. Governments require international monies in order to settle any net imbalance in their aggregate payments account with other countries. A country issuing an international key currency has an appreciable advantage from this point of view, as had the United States in the 1960's. Other governments normally maintain official reserves of foreign money to cover regularly or irregularly recurring deficits. Irregular imbalances can occur as a result of shifts in the demand for a state's exports or of sudden changes in capital movements, crop failures, war, or similar exogenous disturbances. (The other way round, similar factors can produce an accumulation of reserves.) Since the International Monetary Fund may help in the event of serious pressure, many governments tend to maintain smaller reserves of their own than caution requires.

In principle, copious foreign-exchange reserves (or gold) clearly can play a part in exerting or resisting economic pressure. A's foreign-exchange hoard is important if it wants to sell B's currency in order to put that currency under speculative pressure, or if it wants to shift imports from B to a higher-cost exporting country, or if it wants to cut exports to B while unable immediately to find substitute markets. Similarly, B's international currency reserves are an important asset when A cuts off its imports from B, and B does not find satisfactory alternative markets, or if it must pay higher prices in order to replace imports embargoed by A. If B owns insufficient reserves under such circumstances, its industries depending on exports and imports will suffer with possibly multiplying consequences to employment and income; or *B* may have to borrow foreign currency from third countries on possibly unfavorable terms. Not rarely, a weak reserve position will curtail a government's capacity to engage in warfare at home or abroad. In 1956, when Great Britain and France, in collaboration with Israel, attempted to reoccupy the Suez Canal, a precipitate flight from sterling was important among the pressures that brought this military intervention to a quick end, especially since the United States government pointedly refused monetary assistance. In 1971, accumulating balance-of-payments deficits in the United States brought about a negotiated realignment of major currency values, depreciating that of the dollar vis-à-vis the surplus countries. This experience signaled a diminished international ability of the United States to finance the exercise of military power abroad, even though the currency negotiations also reflected the great economic power of the United States in that the results brought great short-term relief and advantage to it. On the other hand, accumulating large international reserves for various emergency purposes, or for strengthening a state's ability to wage economic warfare—contingent purposes that may not arise—is definitely expensive. Hoarding means foregoing the use of the sequestered funds for purchasing imports, and decreased imports mean either less consumption or less investment.

The foregoing analysis indicates how a state can increase its putative economic power generally and vis-à-vis particular countries. It can boost its general economic power by promoting its economic development relative to other states. Japan, which achieved exceptional growth rates throughout the 1960's, clearly had more such power at the end than at the beginning of the decade. However, the degree to which relative economic development enlarges economic power depends crucially on how it affects the structural conditions. Within limits (including costs) imposed by endowment with natural and other productive resources, a state can shift resources so as to lessen its economic dependence on other countries and to increase their economic dependence on itself. Within such limits, it can also cultivate monopolist and monopsonist market power. It can, for instance, develop superior technologies, giving it, at least temporarily, a degree of monopoly over the international supply of certain goods and services.

A state can also attempt to extend its control over resources and markets by forming monopolist or monopsonist arrangements with other states or by becoming the member of a regional bloc or customs union. Thus, states have in the past attempted joint regulation of the international supply of raw materials (e.g. rubber and tin) and are doing so now (e.g. the association of petroleum-exporting countries, sugar, and coffee). Alternatively, groups of private enterprises have set up private international cartels in order to control markets of manufactured products at home and abroad. A currently interesting development of market power is the European Economic Community (EEC) formed by France, Italy, West Germany, and the Benelux countries, which even prior to the probable entry of Great Britain constituted the world's largest territorial unit in international commerce. Such economic integration between states enlarges the size of international economic transactions, which is one determinant of economic power; and it also tends to extend the limits within which the structural requirements of such power can be promoted.

To the extent that schemes for concerting the economic policies of independent states provide a basis for enhanced economic power, this power is, of course, shared and has, as experience shows, a brittle foundation because the diverging interests of members impede cohesion. Member states frequently differ on the merits of particular policies. Cohesion tends to be especially weak when no one member has superior economic size and decisions are made, formally or informally, on the basis of unanimity, for such a configuration maximizes the veto power of each member. Cohesion will tend to be stronger if one member predominates in economic size *and* enjoys a position of leadership or domination based on political, military, or economic power over the other members. The predominant state may then be able to wield the bloc's economic power for its own or for more or less shared purposes. The leading state's ability to decide on this matter is the greater, the less it needs to bargain with (i.e. make concessions to) member states.

In addition to these measures apt to enhance a state's general economic power, it can do things designed to bolster its putative economic power vis-à-vis particular countries. Thus, A can concentrate more on its trade on B, making itself more important to B as an importer and exporter, by giving B preferential access to its market, by offering exports at preferential prices, or on attractive credit conditions, and by offering long-term trade contracts on favorable terms. In doing so, A may pay attention to qualitative factors, as by concentrating on exports for which it has a degree of monopoly power and B's demand is very inelastic, and by concentrating on imports regarding which A enjoys or can build up a degree of monopsony power and for which its demand is elastic. Or A may be able to increase B's dependence by bringing about and exploiting penetration of B's economy by means of fostering direct investment, bribing officials and businessmen in B. Or A may export capital to B on favorable terms and induce a degree of international indebtedness in B that makes it unattractive to other exporters of capital.

The above analysis of the economic bases of economic power implies (and we need not spell out) the various ways by which weak states can attempt to reduce their susceptibility to economic pressures. The over-all purpose of such measures by B will be to diversify participation in competitive international markets for both its exports and imports, to maintain its own competitive standing in these markets, and thus generally to avoid or minimize relations of unequal economic dependence.

In other connections, the existence and consequences of big international and multinational business corporations will claim our attention. For instance, they play a part in the economic penetration of states from outside. Yet they cannot be regarded as a much more than negligible instrument or base of economic power. The vast majority of these firms are American, West

European and Japanese. In the case of private American and West European corporations, governments have no or no more than negligible control over them for purposes of exerting economic power abroad, although governments may apply economic and other power to benefit these firms in their foreign operations. Government control from this point of view will obtain to some extent when governments are part owners of such corporations, and to a greater extent when such corporations are public. In the Japanese case, co-operation between government and business corporations is closer than in the West; there is no evidence, however, of the use of this connection for purposes of wielding economic power.

Finally, the economic domination of one state by another remains to be clarified. Evidently the concept refers not to an occasional relationship but to one which has a degree of continuity over time. As observed above (pp. 77–78), economic dominance resulting from the sheer unintended impact of leading national economies on lesser economies is not economic domination. Nor, it is important to point out and stress, does domination exist just because one state possesses the economic bases of superior economic power over another state. Putative economic power, like putative military power, can become actualized in particular relationships through three mechanisms: (1) A applies economic power purposely for weakening B economically; (2) A applies economic power by threatening B with economic reprisals or by offering economic rewards for compliance with a request by A; (3) B's behavior is influenced by the mere anticipation that, if he pursues actions detrimental to A's interests, A might resort to the exercise of economic power. Clearly, economic domination occurs if A deliberately and regularly resorts to actions identified under (1) and (2). But A's mere ability to take such measures does not involve B's economic domination. The problem is trickier when it comes to the mechanism (3). Clearly, again, once A has had frequent recourse to mechanisms (1) and (2) vis-à-vis B, B may henceforth be dominated by the sheer anticipation of such further acts if he should cross A's interests. This is how continued domination will normally operate. But if B has not been subjected to A's economic power via mechanisms (1) and (2), it will be affected through mechanism (3) only if A, by repeated and recent power plays against other states, has displayed a strong predisposition to resort to its economic power. The less A has displayed such a propensity, the less B will be influenced and dominated by A's economic power. Should A have no such propensity, no influence will occur. In any case, economic domination is strong if A deliberately cultivates the actualization of its economic power vis-à-vis B. Economic domination will be weaker if A has succeeded frequently in actualizing its economic power against C and D, but not against B. Economic domination does not arise at all if A, despite vastly superior "economic strength" suitable as a basis of economic power, lacks any reputation for seeking to exploit this capacity, that is to say, for transforming it into economic power.

Noneconomic Bases of Economic Power

In connection with the concept of economic domination we have just discussed the reputation of a state for exercising national economic power as one basis of such power. The two remaining bases will be taken up briefly, since a fuller explanation would mostly be repeating what has been said earlier about the corresponding bases of military power. The same general factors apply.

It goes almost without saying that skill of government is a critical asset in wielding and accumulating putative economic power. The following abilities are evidently germane: to recognize international opportunities for applying or augmenting economic power; to identify the policies and combinations of policies which will maximize national economic power or economic power potential per unit of effort or costs; to perceive methods for adding to or exercising economic power which are also desirable on other grounds and whose harmful side effects are minimal; especially to recognize and resolve conflict between the rise and build-up of economic power and the application and build-up of military power; to act diplomatically in the use of economic threats and blandishments; to co-ordinate the pertinent activities of different parts of the government and minimize counterproductive behavior by different bureaucracies; to maximize domestic support and minimize domestic opposition to the employment and accumulation of national economic power. In addition, skill is a requirement in all monetary and economic policy which appreciably affects economic growth, foreign trade, and balance-of-payments positions. For example, the relative overvaluation of sterling during the 1920's and again during the 1960's (before 1967) impaired Britain's position as an economic power. All these tasks can be done well or badly, and this affects economic power. Information, analysis, projection, sensitivity to feedback, flexibility, and judgment are the principal means for discharging the administrative jobs with efficiency.

There will be no economic power without the organized will to use "economic strength" for this purpose. As is true of the resort to military strength, government perceptions of the need for, or advantage of, bringing economic power to bear, depend crucially on the emergence of particular interstate situations. But, similar to the corresponding foundations of military power, the following dispositions of society tend to support this will to engage in the active or defensive exercise of economic power. First, the disposition to favor an aggressive use of national power vis-à-vis foreign countries which act to frustrate the pursuit of "national interests." Second, the degree of national solidarity to which governments can appeal in the exercise or build-up of economic power. Third, the disposition to follow the lead of government in matters of foreign policy, including foreign economic policy. Fourth, the support of interest groups expecting sectional benefits from use or augmentation of economic power. Against such support must, of course, be set the opposition of special-interest groups expecting to lose. For example, the opposition of American farm interests has prevented large-scale trade between the United States and the southern countries of Latin America. How much net support will come forth from these sources depends on the distribution of these motivations in terms of influence.

The economic costs of organizing and wielding economic power will naturally tend to reduce support. Sectional and aggregate costs may be distinguished from this viewpoint. Sectional costs, of course, may be balanced more or less by sectional gains. For example, if the government attempts to build up economic power by restructuring the economy along the lines discussed above, the owners of some productive resources will gain relatively to the owners of resources which are depreciated. Similarly, if economic power is applied, for instance by embargoing imports from another country, domestic producers previously competing with these imports will gain, while consumers will lose. The political weight of the gainers and losers depends not only, of course, on the size of the gains and losses. Differences in access to, and exercise of, political influence on government will in large part establish the political weight of the affected interest groups. However, there are two factors which tend to give the advantaged groups a greater incentive to use their political influence than is the case with disadvantaged groups. One factor results from the notorious fact that the disadvantages are often diffused (as in the case of consumer interests), while the advantages are concentrated. The second factor results from the fact that, when the power-oriented policy is contemplated, the likely beneficiaries are frequently more aware of the consequences than are groups which will eventually suffer.

The matter of aggregate net costs (or gains) to society as a whole is extremely complex. Beyond question, the build-up of national economic power entails costs, possibly very considerable, to the extent that it requires policies conflicting with measures to preserve or augment wealth or income. Beyond question also, the wielding of economic power is costly whenever it calls for diverting trade or capital investments from the channels indicated by sheer economic gain. If economic aid is extended in the form of gifts or uneconomic loans, the necessary funds will come one way or another, usually by way of taxes, out of economic surplus above current consumption. Unless unemployed resources can be put to work for the purpose, all costs involve losses in income and, by interfering with the economic allocation of resources and perhaps reducing domestic investment, in a lowering of economic growth. When higher than world prices are paid for imports, or exports are made at prices lower than those prevailing in the world market, worsening terms of trade involve losses in national real income. But the question is whether all parts of society are aware of such costs and, if so, whether these costs are accepted in the expectation, whether justified in retrospect or not, of the ultimate derivation of net national gains from the use of economic power. Whether or not over-all economic gains will actually accrue is an empirical matter; and the expectation of such gain can turn out to be illusory because the exercise of economic power turns out to be more costly and/or less effective than anticipated, or because other intervening conditions inhibit the generation of gains.

The expectation of gain by some groups may, of course, prove realistic even though aggregate losses are incurred, as for instance when groups benefit from doing business with or in a dominated economy. If those groups are part of the elite with powerful influence on government, effective policy support (or demand) will be strong. That, of course, is a matter of sectional gain. However, when the beneficiaries of sectional profit are part of the elite and can bring substantial public influence to bear, they may be in a position to play down the cost side and persuade the public to form illusionary expectations, as has often happened in the acquisition and maintenance of colonial empire. Again, slanted information and evaluation may prove effective as the policy in question is being carried out because the distribution of the accruing costs is diffuse or because the country concerned is experiencing rapid economic growth which, though in fact less than it would have been without the cultivation of economic power, may be attributed to it.

But governments will receive support in the employment of economic power even though no over-all economic gains, or even economic losses, are anticipated as long as compensating non-economic gains are expected and sufficiently appreciated. Such gains can involve various values, for instance a military advantage, or an unsqueamish sense of power, or the satisfaction of punishing a disloyal ally, or plain gratification derived from a quarrelsome or meddlesome international posture. In such cases as well, support of government is determined by who values what and how much, who expects to share in the costs to what extent, and by the distribution of political influence of those calculating in this manner. Again, policy support will diminish as policy is implemented when the accruing gains are less, and the costs incurred more, than expected. Public support is especially apt to wane when the costs are large and salient, as for example, when foreign economic aid is extended. By the 1960's, the American public, and its political representatives, showed increasing fatigue in the matter of foreign aid, and about one-third of all foreign-aid personnel, in Washington and overseas, came to be employed just in preparing supporting materials for presentation to Congress.[3] But even when the economic burden is relatively diffuse, cost consciousness may increase in the public and undermine policy support. This is especially likely if, given the size of the economic surplus, competing demands on its use are pressing hard. Interest groups, representing these competitive claims, will become more sensitive to the cost of using economic power internationally and, whatever their basic access to political influence, will bring it increasingly to bear. Cost consciousness is sensitized, furthermore, when the costs are salient while expected benefits of any kind are uncertain, vague, or even at best exceedingly diffuse. Support for foreign aid is precarious for this reason as well when aid is given to help develop less developed countries. In the United States, weak support of aid has been attributed to the absence of a sizable domestic constituency; and this absence is caused in considerable part by the diffuseness as well as the uncertainty of anticipated benefits. In order to counteract such erosion of public support, government may attempt to curtail the salience of the costs. In the United States, this has been attempted by channeling aid through many different government agencies and thereby impeding Congressional efforts at cutting down total aid appropriations.[4] Finally, changes in the domestic-class balance of power are apt to modify the evaluation of costs and gains at the level of government.

Types of States and Economic Power

Can one associate differences in economic power with kinds of states? The multiplicity of factors affecting national economic power makes it unlikely that simple, clear-cut associations abound. If we begin with the economic base, size and over-all wealth (or degree of economic development) suggest themselves at once as classificatory criteria. And indeed, everything else of importance being the same, one would confidently expect small or poor, and especially small *and* poor, countries as a group to compare as a matter of course unfavorably, as far as the economic base is concerned, with big or rich, and especially big *and* rich countries. These propositions follow readily from the fact that magnitude of foreign economic transactions is important to the economic base for economic power, and that this magnitude is a product of size and wealth. Belgium is rich and Indonesia is poor. Both lack the volume of transactions to sustain considerable economic power. A great economic power must have an outstanding combination of wealth and size. Wealth and a high and rising level of economic development bring other assets. One is versatility of resources and flexibility in the allocation of productive factors, which is an advantage in the management of trade disruptions and of restructuring foreign trade with a view to enhancing economic power. Another is relative ease in the generation of a large economic surplus from which capital and aid exports can be drawn. This is not to say that a poor country is unable to produce a considerable surplus. China does so. But it takes a strong effort and superb organization to restrain private consumption in a poor state; and even with a strong effort, the limit of endurance is reached more quickly than in a highly developed country, and in fact very large size, as in China's case, affords an appreciable base for both economic and military power even at a relatively low level of industrialization. A number of less developed countries have engaged in foreign economic aid. Of these some—e.g. China and Kuwait (a rich underdeveloped country)—have been net exporters of aid, while others —like India, which has given aid to Nepal—are net recipients of aid. But the total amounts involved have been small. Foreign economic aid flows overwhelmingly from more developed states.

Relative economic dependence on the outside world is a matter of resource endowment, level and structure of demand for goods and services, and of commercial policy. National wealth does not *per se* favor *passive* economic power. A very low level of economic dependence on the outside world is indeed easier for a poor agricultural country to achieve. Prior to the industrial revolution, most countries had a low economic dependence on the outside world. Contrariwise, a highly developed and rich country is bound to have large international economic transactions since participation in the international division of labor is a prerequisite to high labor productivity resulting from specialization and economies of scale. As the examples of the Soviet Union and the United States indicate, geographic size tends to increase passive economic power, since large territories are more likely than small ones to possess a variety of mineral deposits, soils, and climatic conditions, and since internal transportation costs tend to impede foreign trade. Trade policy is a third major variable because it can also limit international economic interdependence, as is, for instance, the case with the Soviet Union.

The chief *structural* conditions favoring active or passive economic power involve, as we have seen, imports, which are relatively nonessential and permit a degree of monopsonist power, and exports, which are essential to other states and enjoy a degree of monopolist power. Regarding the essentiality of imports, poor countries, which are self-sufficient in food and clothing, are as a group less vulnerable than rich countries, nearly all of which import vital raw materials, fuel, and semimanufactured and manufactured goods, and whose economies (highly enmeshed with other economies) would suffer profound disruption if not paralysis, if cut off from external supplies. In a sense, Haiti, Madagascar, and China are more self-sufficient than Japan, Great Britain, and Luxembourg. But such generalization does not carry us very far, since there are, of course, striking differences in this respect in both groups. Among the more developed countries, the United States and the Soviet Union are less dependent economically than Japan and West Germany; and among the poorer countries, Singapore is more dependent than Afghanistan. Again, size is a qualifying factor. Moreover, less developed countries, bent on rapid industrialization or in urgent need of modern arms, have greatly advanced their degree of economic dependence. Since many less developed countries are in this position now, they are, it has been said by their spokesmen, more dependent on foreign trade, and their imports less compressible, than is the case with rich countries. Yet there is no evidence to the effect that trade looms larger in relation to national output in the poor than in the rich states.[5] Whether the imports of underdeveloped countries are less compressible is unclear, since need has many determinants which differ in being discretionary. However, if such states, determined on fast economic growth, have eliminated luxury imports and, as a result of previous borrowing for investment purposes, suffer from a large burden of external indebtedness to be serviced, they will have relatively incompressible import requirements. Nevertheless, if highly developed states possess superior flexibility and versatility for adjusting to economic disruption, poorer countries can absorb it by falling back into accustomed poverty for a time and survive. How could Japan or western Europe adjust to an embargo on oil?

Concerning the possession of monopolist or monopsonist advantages, it is clear that monopsonist power is impossible for poor and small states. It takes a big and rich country to account for a large proportion of world imports in any commodity market. On the other hand, the distribution of monopolist advantages shows no regular association with size (in terms of population) and degree of economic development. To be sure, monopolist positions based on rare skill and pioneering technology are possible only in very developed countries. But the latter are at no advantage as a group regarding natural resources. Size, in terms of area rather than population, is once more a modifying factor here. To give some examples of monopolist positions in poor countries, Chile enjoyed a world monopoly in nitrates before World War I. The Congo, Zambia, Chile, and Peru have the bulk of the world's rich copper deposits. The Arab states, Iran, and Venezuela account for the vast bulk of the world's riches in oil. Indeed, in the very important case of petroleum, the monopolist advantages of less developed states are associated with an extraordinarily price-inelastic demand in most of the rich countries. Concerning the noneconomic bases of national economic power, no generalization about the element of will appears supportable. In principle, the more developed countries command a larger supply of relevant skill. But this advantage is decreasing. The supply of these skills does not call for large numbers of experts; and a few experts can be imported or developed through training in the richer states.

Three conditions tend to put the poor countries at some disadvantage compared with rich countries, and these burdens increase their vulnerability to the exertion of economic power. One is the high proportion of primary products in their exports. As a class such exports tend to fluctuate in price and also in volume more than do exports of industrial goods. This fact, often combined with a low price-elasticity of supply, makes export receipts more volatile and causes a weakness when export proceeds slump. This effect is reinforced by the additional fact that the exports of those states are more concentrated, that is, involve fewer commodities, than are the exports of highly developed economies.[6] Finally, even though their export earnings tend to be relatively unstable, less developed countries—other than those with large oil exports—as a group have smaller foreign-exchange reserves in relation to imports than do the highly developed countries as a group.[7]

There is, however, one additional classification of states which has considerable bearing on the bases of national economic power. This involves states operating centralized command economies, usually called Soviet-type economies, versus capitalist states with market-type economies. The effects of geographic and population size and of relative level of development, of course, cut across this distinction. But there are relevant and significant differences in policy and institutions.[8]

First, most countries with Soviet-type economic systems and in particular the Soviet Union and China, have been pursuing trade policies designed to keep foreign trade relatively small in relation to GNP. Unless political conflict interferes, they also tend to favor states with the same fundamental political and economic system. It is clear historically that Communist regimes preferred a degree of self-sufficiency because they were wary of far-reaching economic interdependence with capitalist states; and they were evidently prepared to pay for more autonomy by foregoing the gains obtainable through a greater degree of international specialization (which were not, however, fully understood).[9] This restriction on participation in world trade redounds to these countries' passive economic power; but while it permits less leverage usable against them, it also tends to reduce the leverage they enjoy against other states.

Second, the state has a monopoly over the foreign trade of these countries. This puts their governments in a favorable position to shape the structure of exports and imports within the limits of economic feasibility, to fix export prices lower, and import prices higher, than prices prevailing in world markets, to favor one foreign country over another, and to conclude long-term export and import deals. A state monopoly over foreign trade is also an advantage in using any elements of monopolist and monopsonist power that their exports and imports may enjoy in the world market. In other words, these states enjoy administrative institutions far superior to those of capitalist countries, for waging economic warfare or supporting other countries economically. Third, since countries with Soviet-type economies are usually politically authoritarian, their governments tend to command more political power, than governments in capitalist states, to impose the economic costs of exercising economic power upon their populations. This holds true of the costs of pushing foreign trade into uneconomic channels; and it holds true likewise of their ability to curb private consumption, provide for a large economic surplus, and extend foreign loans and aid. This is not to say that their governments are themselves insensitive to the costs of wielding economic power, because resources employed for these purposes are unavailable for investment or defense. Nor can they be completely indifferent to the economic aspirations of the societies they rule. But, unless the ruling groups are themselves divided on these matters, they do tend to possess incomparable authority regarding the use of economic resources. Fourth, states maintaining Soviet-type economies are remarkably insulated against depressive or inflationary pressures coursing through the rest of the world economy, and, not having freely convertible currencies to begin with, they are also immune against adverse currency speculation.[10] This ability to ward off external economic impulses is rooted in the fact that the economic life of these states is not as organically interlinked with the world economy as are the economies of capitalist countries. On the other hand, Soviet-type economies have not rarely suffered from painful shortfalls in the planned domestic production of essential supplies, and their governments were then compelled to seek relief in world markets. Thus Soviet-type economies have experienced repeatedly drastic shortages in food production resulting in part from their inability to provide collectivized farmers with a proper incentive structure, often in part from slighting agriculture in the allocation of investment, in part from the incompetence of central bureaucracy in dictating farm production, and in part also from basically unfavorable natural conditions (e.g. climate and soil fertility). Thus, the Soviet Union, China, and East Germany have been compelled from time to time to make unusually large imports of food.

The advantages available to states featuring command economies are, of course, significant for economic power only when associated with size and a fairly high degree of economic development, or when they act in concert. By themselves, Bulgaria and Albania fail in size from this point of view. The Soviet Union has such a base, and China's will grow as she becomes more developed. Whether the institutional assets of these states are used for exercising economic power is, of course, a matter of will which, as mentioned, is affected by the opportunity costs of doing so. Nazi Germany, which possessed some of these advantages of a command economy (e.g. state trading), although remaining formally capitalist, engaged in large-scale application of economic power—especially vis-à-vis the primarily agricultural countries of Eastern Europe—and, incidentally, was greatly assisted in doing so by the Great Depression of the 1930s.[11] The Nazi government evidently had the necessary will. However, as will be seen in chapter 6, the Communist states have not made extensive use of their institutional advantage for applying economic power.

Some Conclusions

Like all power, national economic power is relative. It is relative to the economic needs and vulnerabilities of other countries. And, furthermore, great economic power can be balanced by economic counterpower. Moreover, the significance of the international distribution of economic power depends on the international distribution of other kinds of power and influence, including military strength. After all, a state pressed by adverse economic power might seek relief by resort to military power. However, on the whole the two patterns of power distribution do not grossly diverge. This is so because size is an asset behind either form of power, and so is economic capacity. To be sure, the economic strength suitable to underpinning military and economic power is not the same. But there is substantial overlap. The United States and the Soviet Union are the top military powers. The former is also the supreme economic power, and the latter is surely also among the leading economic powers.

Is there in fact an international balance of economic power, as there is a balance of military power? Some writers deny this.[12] Such views rest on the assumption that national wealth and economic power are the same, and on the attendant failure to distinguish between co-operative nonzero-sum and conflictive nonzero-sum uses of economic resources. It may be practically difficult to measure and compare the economic power of states. But rough approximations are feasible in principle.

In the past, the economic wealth and power of states have undergone frequent and substantial changes mostly as a consequence of conquest, and of economic growth in some, and of economic decay in other areas. The histories of the Ottoman Empire and of Spain are as striking examples of decay as that of Japan since the Meiji Restoration is one of almost fabulous economic rise. The power of England, the first "workshop of the world," declined as newcomers joined the ranks of industrial states. Future differences in economic development alone are bound to modify the present international balance of economic power. Imagine the impact if China, given her large and growing population, manages two or three decades of rapid industrialization. The economic growth of any of the larger societies now comparatively underdeveloped will make itself felt in the world's power balance unless rapid economic advance entails disunity and instability, as frequently tends to happen under conditions of swift change. Consolidation of states could likewise alter the world map of economic power greatly. This could happen if the EEC, possibly joined by Britain and some smaller European countries, achieved tighter political as well as economic integration.

And then, of course, there could be disturbing shifts in economic (as well as other kinds of power) resulting from changes in the political and cultural conditions that affect the will to apply power. As was observed in chapter 3 concerning military power, current changes taking place in the affluent Western societies may profoundly affect their ability to muster and utilize power of any kind.

Notes

1. François Perroux, *L'economie du xxeme siècle* (Paris: Presses Universitaires, 1961), pp. 27–56.

2. The best literature on these instruments includes Albert O. Hirschman, *National Power and the Structure of Foreign Trade* (Berkeley: University of California Press, 1945); Peter Bernholz, *Aussenpolitik und Internationale Wirtschaftsbeziehungen* (Frankfurt a. Main: Klostermann, 1966); Yuan-li Wu, *Economic Warfare* (New York: Prentice-Hall, 1952); P. J. D. Wiles, *Communist International Economics* (New York: Praeger, 1968), especially chap. XVI.

3. John D. Montgomery, *The Politics of Foreign Aid* (New York: Praeger, 1962), p. 218.

4. David A. Baldwin, *Economic Development and American Foreign Policy, 1943–62* (Chicago: University of Chicago Press, 1966), p. 270.

5. A. I. MacBean, *Export Instability and Economic Development* (Cambridge, Mass.: Harvard University Press, 1966), pp. 89–107.

6. Michael Michaely, *Concentration in International Trade* (Amsterdam: North Holland Publishing Co., 1962), p. 16.

7. Cf. June Flanders, *The Demand for International Reserves* (Princeton: Princeton University Press Studies in International Finance No. 27, 1971), esp. pp. 12–17, 34–42.

8. For the best analysis of these differences, see Wiles, *Communist International Economics, passim.*

9. Cf. Frederick L. Pryor, *The Communist Foreign Trade System* (Cambridge, Mass.: MIT Press, 1963), chap. I.

10. For a penetrating examination of the agricultural problem in the Soviet Union, see Erich Strauss, *Soviet Agriculture in Perspective: A Study of Its Successes and Failures* (New York: Praeger, 1969).

11. For an excellent analysis of this experience, see Hirschmann, *National Power and the Structure of Foreign Trade*, pp. 34–39.

12. Charles P. Kindleberger, *Power and Money* (New York, Basic Books, 1970), p. 69.

CHAPTER

5

The Uses of Military Power

In its first part, the present chapter develops a theory of the conditions determining decisions to go to war or to apply military threats, explains the impact of modern technology on the usability of force, and explores several factors that have tended to diminish the utility of military power in the contemporary world. The second part discusses the great variety of goals in support of which military power has been wielded in the past, paying special attention to the pursuit of economic gains, and ends with a critique of the Leninist theory of imperialism.

Since the uses of military power have received considerable analytical attention in the literature,[1] they will be treated here more briefly than the uses of national economic power. The nature of military power has been examined in Chapter 1 and the bases of military strength in Chapter 3. The principal focus here will be on the general purposes for which national military power has been sought, and on the kinds of objectives and motivations that have led to its use. A secondary focus will be on the conditions, operating in the contemporary world, which affect the usability of force between states.

There are statistical indications which suggest that interstate war has declined in frequency and in great-power participation since World War II.[2] But it is too early to tell whether this change amounts to an enduring secular trend. The use of military force in battle does continue, and there has been a dramatic rise in world military expenditures in recent decades.[3] It has been estimated that these outlays came to $204 billion in 1970, while they were, in 1970 prices, only around $50 billion in 1937. It would not be particularly meaningful to assume that military expenditures at this level are irrational, at least as long as the world is politically and militarily organized as it has been and as it is at the present time. The virtually complete participation of all governments precludes such an easy explanation. The safer assumption is that governments that make these expenditures have apparently little effective choice.

The General Purposes of Military Power

Disregarding, in line with our main focus, domestic requirements and pressures that generate the allocation of substantial resources to the military sector of states, what outward-directed purposes motivate the building and maintaining of military strength? Deferring until now a discussion of the concrete goals and objectives on behalf of which national military power may be applied, we first note that its instrumental use is either protective or aggressive. Use is aggressive when military power is employed toward altering the relevant *status quo* by force or its threat. Using military power protectively means ultimately either deterring its aggressive use by another actor, or being prepared, should deterrence fail, to defend against the other's attack. Instrumentally, deterrence is essentially coercive. The would-be aggressor is told: If you attack me, I will punish you. The threat of punishment is to influence the behavior of the potential aggressor. Defense can functionally mean either denying success to the aggressor—denial being simply the consequences of action which, if successful, succeeds without affecting the aggressor's intentions except to frustrate them—or coercion in terms of, having hurt the aggressor, holding out further damage to him should hostilities continue, and expecting him for this reason to change his course of action. Similarly, the mere military threat of the aggressor is pure coercion. He hopes to make the defender comply without resort to physical hostilities. On the other hand, should the threat be defied and war ensue, the aggressor's action may be functionally commingled. He may simply overcome the defenses of the attacked actor, but not attempt to coerce him into compliance; or the attacker hopes that the losses inflicted on the defender, presaging further losses and defeat should hostilities go on, will make him quit.

The military threat and its execution represent the first two mechanisms through which putative military power can be actualized, as was explained in Chapter 1. The third mechanism involves the anticipation by the weaker actor that, in the event of a crisis with the militarily stronger state, his deterrent power would probably fail; and that, in the event of military attack, his ability to stop the attack would probably prove insufficient. He therefore prefers to accommodate the stronger actor, avoiding any acute conflict of interest apt to lead to a serious crisis and to the risk of a military threat or war. He bows before the imputed military might of the stronger state; and that might is actualized as the weaker state quietly restricts its behavior. This is when military power works at its cheapest.

Trends in the Usability of Force

In the contemporary world, the military application of nuclear technology has brought about weapons of enormously magnified reach, velocity, and destructive power and, so far at least, also a decisive superiority of offensive over defensive arms on the nuclear level. Under these circumstances, there are no conceivable stakes of conflict which would make all-out nuclear war worthwhile to a rational government, and the risk that lesser conflicts could escalate to the level of massive mutual destruction counsels nuclear powers to avoid any direct military confrontation between one another. This development has reduced the utility of resort to force except for purposes of deterring nuclear attack.

Other factors are currently operating in the same direction. One involves the hobbling of great military power by great and adversary counterpower. No novel phenomenon, this effect of particular constellations of power has appeared repeatedly in the past. But it also has been permeated and has been given a peculiar poignancy by the appalling destructiveness of modern weapons. In any global or regional system of states, the utility of military superiority versus lesser powers (and, conversely, the disutility of military inferiority vis-à-vis greater powers) depends upon the posture that the great powers assume toward one another. Great powers will tend to derive much less utility from their superiority if they contest each other throughout the interstate system. It is not that, in this event, military power is futile. States do extract benefit if checking the influence of other great powers is valuable to them. It is only the reward of power vis-à-vis inferior states which then suffers because the other great power tends to interpose itself. Bipolarity in terms of putative military power has characterized the international system since World War II. But observed difficulty of actualizing superior putative power versus lesser states has tended to make the actual influence structure far more diffuse and less bipolar, and has encouraged polycentric perturbations. The lesser states have been more secure, for this reason as well as others, than used to be the case in previous ages, except in limited areas where one superpower tacitly recognizes the other to be supreme (e.g. Eastern Europe). Hence the not infrequent spectacle of small states defying a great power with remarkable impunity. In short, as in all power situations, including situations of market power, competition between big powers works to the benefit of the weak.

A third condition restricting the utility of interstate force results from the normative devaluation of war. War is no longer the legitimate activity it once was. The UN Charter forbids war except in self-defense, and in support of the victim of aggression. Premeditated attack is thus formally a crime. Customary international norms are less restrictive than law. They likewise proscribe military aggression but seem to permit wars of national liberation and, more vaguely, war to achieve some universal benefit such as a peaceful global community.[4] These new international norms are not very effective. International law, unlike domestic law, is not provided with adequate means of judiciary application and enforcement. It lacks solid authenticity. The new norms, furthermore, suffer from prodigious ambiguities of meaning and of the realities to which they are meant to apply. Despite repeated tries, the United Nations has been unable to formulate a clear-cut acceptable definition of military aggression; and such notions as wars of "national liberation," let alone wars-to-end-wars systems, are exceedingly sensitive to controversial ideological fixations. Moreover, the hold of these norms is rather infirm. Governments, elites, and publics vary in the degree to which they have internalized them, accept them as external prescription, or pay lip service to them. Nevertheless, they are not ineffective either. Compared with the world before World War I, governments behave differently toward the phenomenon of war. If they participate in it, and particularly if they initiate war, they take pains to embellish their motives and go through elaborate efforts of justification. They do not wish to appear warlike.

Military Power and Goal Achievement

This volume will concern itself only selectively with the vast and complex subject of the *causation of war*.[5] We will assume that, whatever else impels man to go to war, or to tread the path leading to it, in doing so, he is also seeking the achievement of

certain objectives, whether to acquire or defend objects of value
to him. We do not deny, for we simply do not possess sufficient
knowledge to the contrary, that man may be genetically designed
to employ intraspecific violence on behalf of goals functionally important to him. Nor do we deny that hostility generated by the
personal frustrations of civilization may not be directed, via the
psychological mechanism of displacement, on to alien actors to
which culture does not usually extend the normative protection
accorded to (often no doubt more deserving) domestic targets
nearby. Indeed, war, and aggressive behavior leading to it, may
well serve to discharge pent-up hostilities (as well as to suspend
temporarily the routine boredom of social life). We do not even
rule out the possibility that such factors of tension relief have acted
as the predominant cause in the genesis of *some* intercommunity
conflicts. This is one reason why actor rationality tends to become degraded. But we assume that the contribution of these
factors is commonly less decisive than the achievement of specific
goals; that is to say, these psychological pressures on individuals
would not have produced military conflict without becoming
attached to goal-oriented behavior.

However, purposive goal seeking need not be essentially outward-directed in order to generate military interstate conflict. International war may figure as a means to the achievement of
domestic goals. Thus, war may be sought by a shaky elite in order
to augment national solidarity, and thereby its own domestic security, or it may be precipitated by a counterelite in the hope of
further dividing society and weakening the elite in power. Or it
may be brought about by the military and armaments producers
in order to safeguard or increase their domestic position and their
claim to a large share of national resources. In fact, inward-
directed and outward-directed goal striving often operates simultaneously, insuring a coalition with sufficient domestic power
to permit the launching of an aggressive policy, and whether the
one or the other dominated in particular instances may remain
controversial even after considerable study. For example, the

aggressive behavior of Germany's elites leading up to World War I can be attributed primarily to their desire to resist rising democratic forces and pressures at home.[6] From the viewpoint of the national actors concerned, the achievement of domestic goals by recourse to external war or its threat will be perfectly rational, provided the use of these means is an effective instrument in its international as well as domestic consequences. If the external war is lost, the achievement of the domestic goals is apt to be doomed or to have lost in value. The attempted achievement of such domestic goals by the cultivation of external conflict may not, of course, be rational from the standpoint of groups which do not share these goals or are opposed to them. But these domestic cleavages in national goal striving do not concern us at this point, the basic problem having been examined in Chapter 2. In any case the question of who wants, pays, and gets what applies as much to outward-directed goals.

To the extent that national goal seeking by resort to international military power is outward-directed, that is, concerned with acquiring something of value under the control of another state, or with preserving possession of something of value coveted by a foreign actor, there are virtually no values of concern to governments that have not been involved in the genesis of war at one time or another. The specific goals may concern military, economic, political or religious (ideological) values of one kind or another; they concern intangible values, such as international prestige, as well as tangible objects of values, such as territory. Any kind of human interest which conflicts with the interests of foreigners and which can be expressed in a proper demand for international action by government is a possible source of contribution to war; and the interests of governments themselves, and of elites they represent, or lean on politically, are of course especially efficacious sources. And it often happens that more than one goal is involved in a particular case. This is a probable first, because different people with influence differ in their goals and preferences, or in the combination of goals they are after;

and second, because some combination of goals is more likely than a single goal to attract sufficient domestic support for any particular application of national military power.

The fact that objectives and hence motivation are frequently mixed is one reason why it tends to be difficult historically to attribute a particular military power play, or the outbreak of a particular war, to a single or dominant concrete objective. A second reason for this difficulty springs from the well-documented fact that actors cannot be counted upon to specify the goals that actually propelled them. If they declare their support for a policy envisaging the use of military force, they are likely to mention more than one objective. They may deceptively stress a particular aim because they deem it more potent in attracting public support. Moreover, they may not know themselves the true structure of their motives. They may wish to deceive themselves because, under the influence of international normative values, they find it preferable to identify with goals regarding which these norms are permissive rather than inhibiting. Third, the motivational origin of war is often obscured by incidental events that lend themselves to its precipitation and often become the official pretext for a belligerent policy (e.g. the assassination of Archduke Ferdinand in Sarajevo, which "precipitated" World War I). Finally, the official war or peace aims of belligerent states may have little to do with the causes of war. As hostilities irrupt and proceed, domestic groups and governments are apt to acquire new reasons for pressing a war to a victorious conclusion, and for exploiting victory; and these new objectives may be quite different from those which brought a state into a particular war. All attempts to reduce the causes of war in general, or of a particular war, to one single or predominant motive are for these reasons hard, if not impossible, to provide with a convincing empirical foundation. To establish the weight of a specific motive or goal in the generation of a particular war, it is necessary to describe exactly how this "cause" had so important an impact, and to describe exactly why other "causes," also present, did not produce this consequence. Historical reality is commonly too refractory to permit such neat

demonstrations. War is an event in whose generation many variable conditions interact. The "seamless web," to which reference
is customarily made, is not a farfetched metaphor.

The "Economic Causation" of War

In any immediate sense, of course, the cause of war can only be
political. It is through the political process, whatever the ultimate
motivations at work, and through government decisions that acts
of war, or acts leading to war, come about. True to the metaphor
of the "seamless web," economic factors and considerations affect
the causation of war in several indirect ways. For one, the ability
to wage war, surely connected with the decision to wage it, rests
on economic foundations. Indeed, organized human warfare could
not arise before primitive societies were able to produce enough of
an economic surplus to release the necessary resources for waging
war. Hence the disposition to conquer control over more economic resources for the purpose of enlarging a society is military
strength. Do we have an economic cause at work in that event?
Or is an economic cause at work only if the increment in military strength is desired in order, subsequently, to wrest economic
assets from other states, or to keep the latter from capturing economic assets one controls? The economic base of military power is
only an example of a larger class of relationships in which economic resources are instrumental to the achievement or enjoyment of other values. Thus, the spread of a religion or political
ideology is facilitated by the use of material resources, especially
if war is used as a mechanism of conversion. The only logical way
to cut into these interdependencies, it seems to me, is to regard
motives as "economic" when they have the acquisition or reten-
tion of economic resources or assets as their motivating objective,
regardless of what the increments of economic income or wealth
are to be used for, or will be used for subsequently. It is understood that there is a difference between motivation and goal,

especially declared goals. The goal may be territorial conquest. The motivation for wanting it may be economic, strategic, ideological, or political (including the political motivation of using external aggression in order to appease domestic unrest), or a mixture of several motivations.

It must be emphasized that the "economic causes of war" are not singled out in the following because of an underlying belief that they are and have been the most important causes, let alone that they are the sole operative cause to which all other "causes" are subsidiary. To be sure, most things valued by man require some economic base. Indeed, historically speaking, before human communities produced an economic surplus composed of resources unclaimed for sheer physiological survival, there was no economic base for creating public goods such as organized government, religious service, judiciary system, arts and letters, and armies. But it did not and does not generally require military power to provide the necessary economic infrastructure. In fact, whenever military power was used to add to the infrastructure of one state, it was at the expense of some other community. From a global point of view, war is economically destructive. Adding victorious and defeated country together, total economic capacity has declined. To see the economic greed of societies as *the* cause of interstate resorts to military strength distorts reality as much as seeing it as the only prize of domestic politics. Given the complex character of social life, and the obvious fact that money and economic resources, and desire for them, are part of the interconnectedness of capabilities, motives, objectives and actions, it is possible, for someone interested in such simplification to focus on the economic motive and assert it to be the master key. Yet the plain fact is that man appreciates many objects of value, including the exercise of power, for their own sake as well as for their transferability into other values, including wealth.

Nevertheless, military power has clearly been employed on behalf of economic objectives so recurrently throughout history that no examples need be given. They can be found in numerous historical works.

THE WANING UTILITY OF MILITARY POWER AS
A MEANS TO ECONOMIC GAINS

I venture the hypothesis that economic motivation as a cause of war has declined since World War II. Since I doubt the feasibility of convincing statistical proof, I will attempt to establish the proposition deductively from the identification of converging trends capable of accounting plausibly for the postulated result.

World War I ushered in changes in world politics which came to full fruition after World War II. In the immediate aftermath of World War I, to be sure, the events of interest to us continued largely to be produced by long-established state behavior. Germany's former colonies were divided by some of the victors, especially Britain and France, which, after the final breakup of the Ottoman Empire, also claimed overlordship over Iraq and Jordan, Syria and Lebanon. In line with the superficially lofty principles of the newly established League of Nations, these territorial transfers took place formally as mandates. Economic interests were only part of the motivations that induced governments to stake out these new extensions of territorial control. Considerations of international or regional order, and of national power and prestige, were no doubt involved as well. In Italy's somewhat anachronistic conquest of Ethiopia in the mid-1930's, economic considerations were clearly secondary to Mussolini's craving for prestige, in his desire to emulate France and Britain and raise Italy to be the center of a far-flung empire. Economic considerations were uppermost, but far from an exclusive objective, in the aggressive thrust of empire-building by Nazi Germany and Japan. The leaders in both great powers depicted their nations as "Have-Nots" requiring more geographic space—and with it more labor, natural resources, and markets—as due to their status as great powers and indispensable to their economic survival and development.

On the other hand, the interwar period witnessed developments whose full significance was revealed only after World War II. One was the Bolshevist revolution in Russia and its challenge to capitalist imperialism. Another was the Wilsonian notion of national self-determination which generated likewise an anti-imperialist impetus. The establishment of the League of Nations and the Briand-Kellogg Pact of 1928 asserted, however ineffectually, the illegitimacy of aggressive war. The tide of colonial empire was clearly past its crest. Turkey and Saudi Arabia succeeded in maintaining true independence. Iran and Afghanistan were able to shake off overbearing British and Russian influence. The entire Arab world was in a ferment presaging the retreat of European authority. In India, where the first rebellion against Western overlordship had occurred in the mutiny of 1857–1858, the activities of the Indian National Congress and of the Ghandian movement slowly impaired British control.

The world-wide uprising against Western empire and military domination became overwhelming after World War II, which had enormously weakened the imperial powers. The rapid decolonization of the world is too familiar a story to be detailed here. Regarding the wielding of military power in support of national economic objectives, the world is now utterly different from that of 1914 or 1880. The normative devaluation of war as an instrument of aggressive policy has progressed further. The conquest of territory for economic reasons has become an anachronism. In the 1950's, it was still possible for a great power to use military means in order to *defend* economic assets abroad previously acquired (e.g. the Franco-British actions concerning the Suez Canal). But from the viewpoint of the 1970's, these were ill-fated rearguard actions. It would be illogical to employ military force to collect on foreign debts in the age of foreign economic aid.

Two specific factors have combined to account for the present disutility of using force internationally on behalf of economic objectives. One factor, which was analyzed in the foregoing, inheres in the increased difficulty and cost of using military power coercively, let alone of conquering, occupying, and maintaining control over, foreign territory in the age of extra-European nationalism and the anti-imperialist fervor prevailing in the economically less developed lands. The other factor, to which we must now turn, involves a vast, indeed revolutionary, change in the very concept of economic gain obtainable through military aggression.[7] Not only has the cost of such a policy risen steeply, the economic value of the object has diminished close to the vanishing point.

Especially in the economically developed countries, elites have come to understand that domestic savings and investment, including investment in human resources (e.g. education), and advanced technology are the true and potent sources of increased national wealth. The elites in the Communist countries are operating under doctrines to which economic gain derived from appeals to power are clearly anathema, and there is no case of Communist aggression on record which even faintly suggests the presence of economic objectives. In the affluent non-Communist countries, a decisive change in relevant doctrine did not come until after World War II. That change is to be attributed primarily to, first, progress in economics as a social science and, second, the gradual diffusion of a sophisticated economic understanding of reality through higher education. Statesmen who, in their youth, received no or only poor schooling in economics are dying out in the affluent societies. (To illustrate abysmal economic illiteracy of recent governments, one need only point to the attempt of many governments during the great economic depression of the 1930's to cure the economic slump by deflationary policies.) Modern governments are assisted (and partly controlled) by staffs in which economists, and other professionals who are acquainted with economics, are numerous and influential. Above all, the evolution of economic reality over the past three decades has amply reinforced the teaching of economists. The striking and fairly steady increases in national income experienced since World War II, which is unprecedented by the standards of preceding decades, have taken place without colonies, without the use of military power on behalf of economic objectives, precisely as a result of domestic savings, investment, and technological advance. It is ironic in retrospect that Germany and Japan—which brought on World War II in pursuit of empire and were defeated and devastated—have been among the top performers, while, for example, Portugal with its colonial empire still largely intact, remains a comparatively undeveloped and poor country.

Seeking riches abroad by means of violence and military domination is today evidently a thing of the past. Since this change is largely the product of scientific advance which cannot be undone, it seems logical to regard this bit of historical change to be final. Two contingencies, however, cast some doubt on this pleasant expectation regarding the more remote future. First, the ability of advanced countries meagerly endowed with indigenous natural resources (e.g. Germany and Japan) to multiply their national incomes over recent decades rested on the operation of a liberal international trade system. These countries would be seriously discommoded if the current trading system crumbled. The world, and especially the affluent states, is depleting world resources of fuel and other minerals at a stupendous rate. It is not clear whether adaptive technology will permit the progressive substitution of still abundant for increasingly scarce metals and sources of energy rapidly enough to prevent stultifying consequences. Second, the alarming increase of world population forecast on the basis of contemporary trends—e.g. perhaps a doubling by the year 2000—will not only accelerate the depletion of unevenly distributed mineral resources; it could also produce a historical throwback in the form of a very primitive urge of dense populations to seek relief by migration. Whether these contingencies will materialize is, of course, highly speculative at the present time.

THEORIES OF TERRITORIAL IMPERIALISM

In explaining the motivating force of economic interests in military action abroad, it is one paradigmatic view to perceive, as this author does, governments representing the interests of certain elites and sometimes larger publics seeking economic gains abroad by forcible means when these interests reflect primarily economic motives. It is a quite different view to regard certain politicoeconomic systems as propelling such economic aggression *automatically*. The latter view is that of many Marxists and especially Leninists as expressed in their theories of imperialism. Historically, Marxist theories of imperialism have displayed considerable variation around the basic Marxist paradigm. They disagree on the particular economic causes which drive the governments of capitalist states automatically toward imperialism, some seeing an insufficiency of domestic commodity markets as the principal cause, while others single out the insufficiency of domestic opportunities for investing surplus capital. However, the large majority of Marxists, and especially Leninists, insisted on the inevitability of the process.[8]

According to Marxist views, as they evolved during the nineteenth century, the profit striving of private capitalists kept real wages at the lowest possible minimum in the capitalist system. Resulting underconsumption—i.e. the financial inability of the working class to provide a sufficient market for an expanding output of goods and services—doomed the economy inevitably to disequilibrium. It is Lenin's theory that, under mature capitalism, underconsumption is automatically associated with a high propensity to save. Accumulating capital, increasing under monopolist control, faces inadequate opportunities for investment at home. Capitalists, therefore, seek outlets for surplus capital in the less developed world. Colonial dependencies are established there in order to secure such investment outlets in competition with other capitalist states, and in order to assure the safety of investments by the assumption of government authority. As the underdeveloped world is increasingly staked out in this fashion, the imperialist rivalry of capitalist states, rendered especially intense by demands for repartitioning the colonial world on the part of newcomers among capitalist societies, leads inevitably to armed struggle between the imperial powers. Their resulting enfeeblement, in turn, ushers in colonial revolt.

Economic, political, and military events during the half century prior to World War I lent considerable plausibility to Lenin's theory. On the one hand, contrary to the views of the orthodox economists of the time, the economies of the advanced capitalist countries were not assured of fundamental equilibrium through the free play of market forces. The prevailing *laissez-faire* notions of the role of the state in economic affairs and the pre-Keynesian blind spot in macroeconomic insight precluded policies designed to moderate the gyrations of boom and bust. And the high propensity to save, resulting from a grossly unequal division of income, naturally depressed domestic rates of interest and, as the Leninists argued, pushed capital out to seek employment elsewhere. On the other hand, the external behavior of the advanced capitalist states, the larger of which were naturally also the militarily most powerful, also gave appreciable credence to Lenin's thesis. The governments of these countries frequently employed force on behalf of nationals pursuing investment and other businesses abroad; they did engage in a frenzied competitive effort at acquiring colonies, protectorates, and spheres of influence, and, in line with a general retreat from the relatively free-trade policy established at mid-century, they did adopt measures giving their nationals preferential economic access to the empires they had staked out. It is true that World War I did not result from the colonial partition of the underdeveloped world. It was precipitated by Austria-Hungary, Serbia, and Russia, which were hardly seized by mature capitalism. And major squabbles over colonial stakes had been settled by Britain, France, and Germany just before war broke out. But a world war *could* have irrupted at the time as a consequence of imperial expansion. Several times between 1890 and 1914, the great powers came very close to it.

Yet a closer look at this "age of imperialism" reveals gaping discrepancies between historical reality and Lenin's explanatory claim. We will not present a detailed critique of his doctrine. This has been done many times.[9] The principal points of criticism, however, are worth stating in a book on the political economy of international power and influence, especially since the doctrine remains part of the official credo in Communist societies, and since there seems to have been a resurgence of adherence to it in other parts of the world.

Imperialism is a process by which a state conquers or otherwise subdues, and then over time dominates, another country or foreign population. Empire, then, is the exercise of power, usually military, for placing and maintaining foreign populations in a status of subordination. The purpose for doing so depends on the needs and wants of governments and elites in the imperial state.

To acquire and maintain empire involves various and variable costs to the imperial power as well as to the subjugated population. Military and police casualties and parts of defense budgets are incurred in conquering and protecting imperial possessions against colonial rebellion and the contingent or actual challenge of rival foreign powers. Diplomatic relations with other states are apt to be burdened for the same reasons. Costs of administration accrue at home and in the imperial possessions. The economic relationships are a burden on the metropolitan country if preferential arrangements protect inefficient production and make economic transactions diverge from patterns indicated by comparative economic advantage. In terms of domestic politics, the political influence of groups, which are special beneficiaries of the imperial connection, may be magnified to the detriment of other groups in the imperial country. Finally, depending on the normative environment at home and abroad, there may be considerable moral costs. What gains, if any, accrue from empire are evidently net gains; and though there be net beneficiaries in the imperial elites, empire may well be a net disadvantage for the population of the imperial country as a whole.

The tracks of history make it abundantly clear that the advantages sought in securing and maintaining empire have been extraordinarily manifold. The glory of monarchs and generals, addiction to political aggrandizement, the propagation of religious faiths, the arrogance of assuming the white man's burden of administering to the benighted races, military security and advantage, diversion from the troubles of domestic politics, prospects of rapid career advancement, and the sheer pleasures of adventure and escape from the restrictive routines of domestic life have all played their part in generating the imperial motivation. Even Joseph A. Schumpeter's thesis of an essentially "objectless disposition," driving a state to ceaseless imperial activity and expansion once the requisite military-administrative machine has been formed (originally often in defensive response to foreign imperialist pressure), and insists on its employment, has considerable explanatory power.[10] And in no case is the effective motivation unmixed, if only because only avidity for diverse advantages will normally assure sufficient political backing in the imperial society. Yet, the annals of history make it equally clear that various economic gains—the acquisition of slaves and other booty, tribute and taxes, sources of raw materials and other goods, sheltered export markets, safe opportunities for investment—have played a major or dominant part in the majority of cases. Moreover, empire meant sectional profit not only as a result of economic transactions in and with the dependencies, but also in the metropolis itself, for those engaged in building ships and producing military supplies and services.

It has been a standard criticism of Lenin's theory that it explains neither preindustrial imperialism nor imperialist strivings in recent decades. This criticism is in part inappropriate, and in part unfair. The Marxists were not only aware of earlier forms of imperialism, Karl Marx himself and others brilliantly contributed to the understanding of these earlier phenomena.[11] Believing in historical evolution by stages, they regarded *modern* imperialism, as the title of Lenin's famous work indicates, as pertaining to "the highest stage of capitalism." On the other hand, there could be no postcapitalist imperialism for Lenin, since he assumed the inevitable downfall of the capitalist order to be followed, via the transitional dictatorship of the proletariat, by purely socialist communities which would live together in natural harmony. When no one could be exploited, empire was logically pointless and impossible. Lenin did not foresee the far from harmonious relations between communist *states* as they evolved after World War II,[12] nor the contemporary forces which, if continuing to grow, could be the makings of all sorts of millennial imperialism. But this failing is common to all prognosticators.

Seriously at fault in Lenin's theory of imperialism is his reduction of all imperial motivations to a single "cause" inherent in the inevitable requirements of monopolist capitalism. His work, first published in 1917, was preceded by J. A. Hobson's *Imperialism* (1902) which was studied by Lenin.[13] Hobson also saw low wages and consequent underconsumption as the most critical cause operating in the colonial scramble preceding World War I. But his theory contained two ingredients which made it analytically far superior to Lenin's work. First, he conceded and described the admixture of all the other, far from insignificant, forces and motives which fed the imperialist drive. Second, he did not regard underconsumption and the imperialist remedy as a necessary property of capitalism; rather he advocated the reform of the capitalist system so as to promote basic equilibrium between aggregate supply and demand in an expanding economy. Both points merit brief discussion.

Any careful scrutiny of the foreign policies pursued by the great powers from 1870 to 1914 suggests very strongly that the statesmen involved in leading positions at crucial times were primarily interested in relative national power and security. To be sure, many of them were active in the drive for extensive colonial empire, and in their country's foreign markets, sources of supply and fields of investment. It is impossible to prove, and indeed implausible on the evidence, that their considerations of power were subordinate and instrumental to considerations of markets and investments. Since the visible evidence is incontestable, the Leninist interpretation must assert that these men, political and military leaders, acted subconsciously as tools of capitalist interests. But this is an assertion which can be neither proven nor disconfirmed with any finality. Its acceptance rests on an act of faith. Evidence on the level of conscious thought and behavior renders it more plausible that national economic interests were subordinate to considerations of relative power and prestige which, in turn, were desired for various combinations of plural ends, sometimes including economic ones.[14] Too often the record shows statesmen using bankers and other businessmen as tools, not rarely reluctant tools, and exploiting these economic interests as pretext for the extension of power.[15] It seems to have been, as Richard Hammond concluded, that it was "emphatically not the case that the Foreign Office or even the Colonial Office in the nineties was chiefly engaged upon economic questions. Their chief concern was playing the good old game of power politics. In that game there were economic moves, of course; there were possibilities of private, as well as public, profit and loss." [16] And in the power game of the time, colonial possessions were regarded as a badge of status. There was an important "international demonstration effect" at work in this respect. Great Britain, the first country to industrialize, was by all odds the premier world power. As other large countries grew industrially, and began to catch up with the United Kingdom, they emulated it. Since Britain sat on top of a far-flung overseas empire, it is no wonder that imperial rule seemed to symbolize great power standing. The imperialist drive of France, Germany, Italy, and (somewhat belatedly and ambivalently) the United States can be said to have involved "prestige imperialism." Even Schumpeter's thesis explains a great deal of this historical reality. In his view, the imperialism of the age was driven essentially by the atavistic and irrational goals and preferences of the European aristocracies and their middle-class imitators, in other words, by precapitalist forces.[17] Barbara Tuchman's vivid portraiture of the leading men makes this interpretation verisimilar.[18] Any theory that tries to reduce a reality as complex as Europe's last imperialist fling to a single causative factor may be elegant in its explanatory simplicity, but is apt to do violence to the known facts.

The Leninist view also presupposes that these countries were governed by one integrated elite, by a "ruling class" which was basically monolithic in its aspirations and united in serving the alleged requirements of the capitalist system. Again, the evidence suggests strongly that, in all the leading states, there was a pluralist elite structure characterized by symbiotic relationships, to be sure, but not by unity of outlook and objectives. Elite interests were more sectional than class interests. In fact, their sectional interests often clashed, and even when they did not, this often resulted from complementarity rather than identity. Lenin needed a theory of capitalized imperialism as part of a powerful anticapitalist ideology, in turn required as a means to achieving revolutionary power. Such militant ideologies demand strong and simplistic beliefs. The carefully qualified and compromised views of John A. Hobson would have been unsuitable for this purpose. As Hugh Stretton has brilliantly pointed out, Lenin picked his theory to serve his political purpose just as others criticized him in order to serve *theirs*. Schumpeter, for example, was interested in exonerating the capitalist system, which, in its pure form, unadulterated by the atavistic forces of the traditional past, he judged to be magnificently creative.[19]

Regarding the inevitable nature of mature capitalism to demand empires, Lenin's belief had to assume that the capitalist system of his age was incapable of change. We owe it to John Strachey to call attention to a critical passage in Lenin's work:

It goes without saying that if capitalism could develop agriculture, which to-day lags far behind industry everywhere, if it could raise the standard of living of the masses, who are everywhere still poverty-stricken and underfed . . . there could be no talk of a superfluity of capital. This "argument" the petit bourgeois critics of capitalism advance on every occasion. But if capitalism did these things it would not be capitalism; for uneven development and wretched conditions of the masses are the fundamental and inevitable conditions and premises of this mode of production.[20]

It can hardly be said that *"capitalism"* reformed itself in the half century after Lenin's book appeared. But the societies in which the capitalist system thrived did enforce reforms via the political process which led to a spectacular rise of real wages and the shedding of imperial possessions while private ownership in the means of production largely continued. Whether we want to call the modified system capitalist or not is a semantic matter. By the 1970's, the affluent societies of the West, and also Japan, do trade and invest abroad, especially among themselves; and in their transactions with less developed countries, they may profit from asymmetries of influence and wealth. But they suffer from no perennial surplus of capital and they do not need or use military power for economic gain derived from abroad. The flag no longer follows trade, and trade no longer follows the flag.

Notes

1. Cf. Quincy Wright, *A Study of War*, abridged ed. (Chicago: University of Chicago Press, 1964); Robert E. Osgood and Robert W. Tucker, *Force, Order and Justice* (Baltimore: Johns Hopkins, 1967); Glenn H. Snyder, *Deterrence and Defense* (Princeton: Princeton University Press, 1961); Thomas C. Schelling, *Arms and Influence* (New Haven: Yale University Press, 1966); Oran R. Young, *The Politics of Force* (Princeton: Princeton University Press, 1968); Klaus Knorr, *On the Uses of Military Power in the Nuclear Age* (Princeton: Princeton University Press, 1966); Klaus Knorr, *Military Power and Potential* (Lexington, Mass.: Heath, 1970), chap. I.

2. David Wood, *Conflict in the Twentieth Century*, (London: Institute of Strategic Studies, Adelphi Papers No. 48, June 1968).

3. The data in this section are from United States Arms Control and Disarmament Agency, *World Military Expenditures 1970* (Washington: 1970).

4. Kjell Goldmann, *International Norms and War between States* (Stockholm: Laromedels forlagen, 1971), p. 210.

5. For excellent introductions, see Dean G. Pruitt and Richard C. Snyder (eds.), *Theory and Research on the Causes of War* (Englewood Cliffs, N.J.: Prentice-Hall, 1969), pp. 1–32; Quincy Wright, *A Study of War*, chaps. V and XXI. Useful also is Herbert A. Simon, "Causation," *International Encyclopedia of the Social Sciences* (New York: Free Press, 1968), Vol. II, pp. 350–355.

6. Eckart Kehr, *Schlachtflottenbau und Parteipolitik, 1894–1901* (Berlin: Emil Ebering, 1930).

7. See Knorr, *On the Uses of Military Power in the Nuclear Age,* chap. II.

8. Vladimir I. Lenin, *Imperialism: The Highest Stage of Capitalism* (Moscow: Foreign Languages Publishing House, 1947). The book was first published in 1917.

9. For some good critiques, see Hans Daalder, "Imperialism," *International Encyclopedia of the Social Sciences* (New York: Macmillan, 1968), Vol. 7, pp. 101–108; Lionel Robbins, *The Economic Causes of War* (London, Jonathan Cape, 1939); John Strachey, *The End of Empire* (New York: Praeger, 1959); Raymond Aron, *Peace and War, A Theory of International Relations* (New York: Doubleday, 1966, chap. IX); George Lichtheim, *Imperialism* (New York: Praeger, 1971), especially chaps. 7 and 8.

10. Joseph A. Schumpeter, *Imperialism and Social Classes* (New York: Kelley, 1951).

11. Cf. Strachey, *The End of Empire,* Part III.

12. R. N. Berki, "On Marxian Thought and the Problem of International Relations," *World Politics* XXIV (1971): 80–105.

13. John A. Hobson, *Imperialism* (London: Allen and Unwin, 1902).

14. R. G. Hawtrey, *The Economics of Sovereignty* (London: Longmans, Green, 1930), chap. V.

15. Staley, *War and the Private Investor, passim.*

16. Richard J. Hammond, "Imperialism: Sidelights on a Stereotype," *The Journal of Economic History* 21 (1961): 595–596.

17. *Ibid.*

18. Barbara Tuchman, *The Guns of August* (New York: Dell, 1963).

19. Hugh Stretton, *The Political Sciences* (New York: Basic Books, 1969), chap. IV.

20. John Strachey, *The End of Empire,* p. 110.

CHAPTER

6

The Uses of Economic Power (I)

The bases and instrumentation of national economic power were described in Chapter 4. We now turn to these instrumental uses in the pursuit of various foreign-policy goals and objectives; we shall examine types of application that have been cultivated frequently in recent decades, and evaluate, as far as possible, the effectiveness of the means involved in the achievement of national ends.

Means and Ends

As described in Chapter 4, the use of national economic power can take many forms, and can serve, or at least can be designed to serve, directly or indirectly, a substantial spectrum of national ends. By resorting to economic power, governments seek the gain or preservation of military, political, ideological, and even emotional as well as economic values. To whom such advantages accrue, or are meant to accrue, in the state wielding economic power—the problem examined in Chapter 4—does not concern us here. All we posit is that governments designate certain objectives and goals as part of national foreign policy, and that they employ means at their command on their behalf. In the following, we will first indicate very briefly a classification of typical *goals* in support of which economic power has been exercised by states and then examine in more detail the use of particular *instruments* of national economic power. The relevant goals of government fall into the following groups.

The Extraction of Economic Gain. We are here concerned with other means than mutually satisfactory exchanges. For instance, during the severe worldwide depression of business in the 1930's, many governments employed quantitative import restrictions and foreign-exchange control in order to raise domestic employment by limiting foreign access to their markets—measures which were called appropriately "beggar-my-neighbor" policies. To give another example, with the consumption of oil rising strongly in the affluent importing countries, and with a demand very inelastic to price changes, the oil producing countries—which had formed a monopolistic organization (the Organization of the Petroleum Exporting Countries—OPEC)—achieved unprecedentedly sharp increases in their revenues from the oil companies by threatening to cut off companies which would fail to conform to their demands. The companies gave in, and the revenues of the producing countries will rise from $7 billion in 1970 to $18.5 billion by 1975. (Without the new terms, revenues would have increased to $10 billion by 1975.) [1]

The Achievement of a Degree of Control over Other States. For example, when Yugoslavia asserted its independence from Moscow's control in 1948, the Soviet government put her under gradually tightening economic pressure by recalling Soviet technical experts, by reneging on a loan agreement, and finally by cutting off all trade and aid with the apostate Communist country. The other Communist states in Eastern Europe followed suit. At the time, more than half of Yugoslavia's trade was conducted with the Communist countries, and she was completely dependent on them for technical assistance and credits. [2] In 1952 the United States condemned the military intervention by Britain and France in Egypt to recover control of the Suez Canal. Great Britain came under increasing monetary pressure as holders of sterling

accounts, fearing a devaluation of the pound, rushed to convert
their balances into gold and dollars. The United States blocked
any aid from the International Monetary Fund and promised help
only after the British government had accepted a cease-fire super-
vised by the United Nations.[3] In order to curb United States deliveries of military aircraft to Israel in 1972, the Egyptian foreign
minister threatened to restrict the sale of Arab oil to American oil
companies which contributed around $2 million to the United
States balance-of-payments receipts.[4]

Throughout history, economic penetration of weak countries
has paved the way to foreign political as well as economic control,
if not outright domination or conquest. Several forms of economic
power have been exploited for this purpose, for instance, by
governments of the advanced capitalist states during the half century preceding World War I. Thus, the purchase of bonds from
less developed countries was a favorite device. When the rising
indebtedness of these countries precluded borrowing elsewhere,
dependence often became complete. Bonds served to "pave the
way for bayonets." [5] Direct investment in ownership and management control of economic enterprise in such states was also
used for the same purpose; and bribery of government officials
played a part in this process of financial penetration which not
rarely led to subjugation.[6] Before World War I, the United
States achieved a high degree of financial and economic penetration in the Caribbean and Central America; and Nazi Germany,
during the middle 1930's in Hungary, Bulgaria, Rumania, and
parts of South America, used the same tactics.[7] After World War II,
the Soviet Union set up joint stock companies, with the local
government as a partner, in the defeated Axis countries Bulgaria, Hungary, East Germany, Rumania, and Austria. Though
on the victorious side during the war, Yugoslavia agreed to the
establishment of two such companies on her territory. These companies had special privileges regarding taxation and foreign-
exchange restrictions. After some experience, the Yugoslav government declared that the "formal parity was only a screen to
conceal direct exploitation." [8] President Tito is reported to have

characterized these stock companies as a means "to enslave us economically."

While the economic penetration of weak states has frequently preceded their formal incorporation into the empire of the strong state, thus entailing a complete loss of sovereignty, economic penetration is also one way for one state to gain prolonged domination—economic and political—over a weaker state which retains its formal sovereignty. The influence of Great Britain over Iran before World War I, and over the Trucial Sheikhdoms until the late 1960's, and of the United States over Panama and Cuba during the first half of this century, are examples of such domination. The degree and scope of control has varied historically a great deal and, in recent decades, and paralleling the decolonization movement the world over, has had a strong tendency to decline and to become more reciprocal and ambiguous. Nevertheless, there exist a great many client-patron relationships in the contemporary world, though the connection is based on various blends of military and economic conditions. The patron typically owes military protection and/or economic and technical aid to the client. At the present time, for instance, France acts as a patron state for most of its former colonies in sub-Saharan Africa, providing financial, technical, and military aid. South Korea, Taiwan and the Philippines have been client states of the United States, Cuba and Finland of the Soviet Union, and Nepal and Bhutan of India. In each instance, there is a marked and prolonged military and/or economic dependence by the client on the patron.

Promotion of National Military Strength. In the late 1960's, the United States paid more than $1 billion in order to maintain 50,000 Korean troops in South Vietnam.[9] It also paid large sums to Thailand for Thai troops to bolster the defenses of Laos.[10] In the 1960's, the extension of financial aid made military bases available for the United States in Spain and elsewhere.

Promotion of the Economic Bases of Military Strength and Economic Power. Thus, foreign investment and economic penetration can be used to acquire and maintain assured access to vital raw materials and fuel supplies abroad. British control over the oil-bearing territories on the Persian Gulf between World Wars I and II served this purpose. Although the movement toward integration in Western Europe (especially the European Economic Community) has multiple political, economic, and military objectives, one of these is certainly the establishment of a broader base for the development of concerted economic power. Indeed, this is a goal of all regional schemes of economic integration.

Promotion of the Capabilities of Friendly and Allied Countries. By means of the Lend-Lease Act of 1941, the United States supplies critical defense goods to countries whose defense was regarded as vital interest. From 1941 to 1945, materials worth nearly $40 billion were transferred, the large bulk to Britain and Soviet Russia. In February 1947, when Britain, owing to her own economic hardships, withdrew financial aid from Turkey and Greece, President Truman obtained Congressional backing for a military-aid program involving $400. When aid of this kind and for these purposes goes to weak countries for lengthy periods of time, the resulting relationship may bring about a patron-client interaction as discussed above.

Weakening the Capabilities of Opponent States. Resorting to economic power for this purpose is, of course, the opposite of using it for strengthening friendly states or governments. The prime example is the United States embargo on the export of "strategic goods" to the Soviet Union and the People's Republic of China. The declared objective is to restrict the military development of these countries.

Symbolizing Displeasure and Inflicting Punishment. Like all power, economic power can be exercised to register displeasure and mete out punishment not for coercive purposes, but simply in order to gratify the actor's emotional desire for hurting a recalcitrant government. Pure examples of this are hard to find, since the power play involved may also be intended to impose coercive pressure. Thus in January 1972, the United States, after having tried in vain to deter India from invading East Pakistan, suspended economic-aid deliveries to India when the latter marched into Bangladesh. A spokesman of the Department of State announced: "The United States is not making a short-term contribution to the Indian economy to make it easier for the Indian government to sustain its military effort." [11] But this act could not have been meant seriously to make India stop in her tracks, and in fact the Indian government lashed out scornfully against the idea that the receipt of American aid would make her subservient to Washington's dictates.[12] The motivation of the American government is not clear from the available record. But it is hard to believe that the action did not arise from a petulant desire to punish and rebuke New Delhi. This was the tenor of speculations in the American press.

Like all power, material economic power can be used for coercion, for influencing the behavior of the weaker actor, or for directly achieving a desired effect, harmful in an adversary relationship, supportive between friendly or allied countries. All of our examples of economic power uses for promoting military strength, the economic bases of military and economic power, for promoting the capabilities of friendly states or governments, and for diminishing the capabilities of opponents involve the noncoercive use of economic power.

Having demonstrated how national economic power can be wielded toward the international attainment of various objectives and ends, we will now concentrate on the analysis of certain uses of economic power that have been historically very important in recent decades. Regarding these uses, a great deal of experience has been accumulated that is relevant to the contemporary world.

Economic Warfare between Belligerents

When modern belligerent states practice economic warfare, they seek to reduce each other's economic base of military (and economic) power relative to their own. In these cases, economic

warfare *supplements* military action as a means to coerce or
simply to overwhelm or resist an adversary. But the immediate
purpose of economic warfare is then not coercive. It is rather to
weaken the economic foundation of the enemy's power. Military
action can, of course, be applied toward destroying the economic
sinews of the opponent's military strength. Naval blockades can
sever trade, and bombing from the air and sabotage on the
ground can destroy factories, shipyards, rail transportation, etc.
In this chapter, however, the focus is on *economic,* not military,
means; and the subject, therefore, is all measures of *economic*
policy designed to enhance one's own economic base relative to
the enemy's.

Historically viewed, economic warfare has been practiced
with considerable frequency, although usually by means of military operations. During the mercantilist age, enemies often traded
with one another but, by striving for a favorable trade balance
(export surplus), attempted to punish the other with a loss of
gold, which was regarded (mistakenly) as the key economic base
of power. Actually, an import surplus increased the opponent's
resources. Napoleon's grandiose Continental Blockade attempted
to break Britain's economic base by cutting all trade with continental Europe. During a half century prior to World War I, when
middle-class power in the main European countries succeeded
for a time in making free trade and unregulated business supreme as a matter of state interest, new laws of warfare, promul-
gated particularly at the Hague conventions of 1899 and 1907,
intended to protect civilian persons and property in time of war
and drastically curtailed the list of contraband articles that
blockading navies were permitted to intercept during hostilities.
World War I witnessed the quick collapse of these conventions as
Britain tried to starve the Central Powers into submission by
cutting off Germany's imports of food and raw materials, and as
Germany in turn attempted to blockade Britain by means of her
submarine force. After World War I, a number of strategists
(among them notably the Italian Giulio Douhet) developed the
idea, sometimes extended to absurd lengths, that economic war

could largely, if not wholly, replace the bloody business of military ground combat as a means to victory. And it was indeed in World War II that economic warfare, pursued by economic as well as military means, was carried on, especially by the United Kingdom and the United States against Germany, on an unprecedented scale and with extreme and ruthless determination.

The principal nonmilitary measures of economic warfare are designed to reduce or terminate the enemy country's imports of critical material in the hope of causing him serious bottlenecks in wartime production, a decline in military equipment and supplies, and, if possible, his economic collapse. Reducing his exports by means of boycotts is a major method for decreasing his ability to import. Export embargoes, export and import quotas, licensing systems, various foreign-exchange and other financial controls, including a freeze of enemy-owned assets abroad, and shipping regulations are the principal techniques of economic warfare.[13] Controlling the foreign trade of neutral countries is naturally the chief problem in waging economic war. In World Wars I and II, Germany's enemies limited exports to neutrals and attempted to restrict their trade with Germany and her allies. Pre-emptive purchasing in neutral states is a major technique for reducing their import by the opponent. Thus, in World War II, the United States and the United Kingdom bought preclusively large amounts of wolfram in Spain and Portugal, and chrome in Turkey, not for use at home but in order to keep them out of Germany.

The rational objective of economic warfare, pursued by economic measures, is not, of course, or should not be, simply to cause maximum losses to the adversary's economic capability. The logic of this type of conflict prescribes that the enemy suffer a maximum reduction of his economic base *relative to one's own.* Simply severing his foreign trade is unlikely to bring this result about. After all, his exports absorb a part of his productive capacity, and their interruption may engender production bottlenecks in one's own economy or in that of allies. The appropriate strategy would interfere with his commerce *selectively* in order to cause maximum *net* impairment to his economy. Clearly, one's own costs must be taken into account. As mentioned, a complete boycott of the enemy's goods may harm one's own side more than his. Moreover, pre-emptive buying is apt to raise prices and be expensive. The implementation of the economic measures involved imposes very heavy administrative costs. Besides, the cost-effectiveness of economic measures should be compared with the efficiency of military acts designed to hurt the enemy's economy. There is, however, a practical reason for eschewing sophisticated applications of economic warfare; and this is the absence of good information and the difficulty of foresight. The data requirements of achieving the best solution cannot be met. This administrative obstacle, therefore, points to cruder operations and an approach to a second-best strategy.[14]

In practice, the effectiveness of economic warfare is difficult, if not impossible, to measure, since the economic policies involved are usually only one factor, and certainly not the weightiest, in determining the outcome of war. Regarding World War II, economic warfare hardly caused the downfall of Germany and Japan, though it contributed to their eventual collapse. And the contribution it did make surely resulted overwhelmingly from *military* measures of economic warfare, from naval blockade, and especially, in the case of Germany, from aerial bombardment.

This conservative appraisal should not be surprising. A resourceful opponent has many ways to minimize and adapt to economic warfare waged against him. He can lay in stock piles of critical materials. He can try to evade the controls imposed on his trade with neutral states. Pre-emptive purchases alone will rarely stop vital imports. For instance, since the above-mentioned buying of wolfram and chrome in the Iberian peninsula and Turkey naturally bid up prices, production was stimulated to expand, and Germany received considerable supplies until nearly the end of the war. The enemy can conquer areas for combined economic and military reasons, as Germany did in World War II. Moreover, he can ration the use of scarce materials or components and eliminate their consumption in the production of less essential goods. He can recycle some scarce materials. If he is technologically resourceful, he will find substitutes for scarce or lacking items. To cite a famous case, in World War I, when Germany was cut off from Chilean nitrates, critical to the production of explosives, her chemists invented a synthetic method of nitrogen production. Of course, all these adjustments are costly (except for innovations that actually reduce production costs). But, in wartime, civilian consumption, at home or in conquered territories, can be made to bear most of the consequences of lowered productivity. Military production may suffer little, or in any case not decisively.

Notwithstanding the large-scale practice of economic warfare by economic measures in World Wars I and II, its utility in the future is uncertain but, in all likelihood, slim if not nil. It is obvious from the preceding analysis that economic warfare is only for large and highly developed belligerents, for it demands a large share in, and potential control over, world trade. A great power at unlimited war with a small one will hardly need economic warfare to subdue it. Moreover, economic warfare makes sense only in the event of a protracted war of attrition. Economic warfare is a game of big powers waging prolonged war against big powers, and this restricts the ranks of possible players in the contemporary world to two: the United States and the Soviet Union (with allies); and even the Soviet Union would have the necessary resources only if economic warfare were conducted by military as well as economic means. Middle powers (such as France and Britain) that can be hardly imagined in the present era to go to war independently, if at all, could not practice economic warfare without backing or tolerance by the United States or the Soviet Union. Given their nuclear capabilities to destroy one another, a war between the United States and the Soviet Union is also virtually unimaginable except by inadvertence. If they should engage in a war which escalated to the strategic nuclear level, nothing could be less relevant than economic warfare. This leaves a protracted limited war between the two great nuclear powers as the only possibility in which the question of economic warfare might arise. Indeed, if such a limited war came about, proved stable in its limitations, and became prolonged, economic warfare would almost certainly play a substantial part. Yet, once again, the possible occurrence of such hostilities, at least at the present time, strains the imagination. Not only would the outbreak of limited war between the superpowers carry with it a strong potential for escalation to the strategic nuclear level, and hence render protraction extremely improbable, the very awareness of this enormous and surely daunting risk on both sides is highly likely, by a process of mutual constraint and self-deterrence, to make them seek avoidance of even a limited military clash as a matter of supreme priority.

Export Embargo on Strategic Goods in Time of Peace

The conduct of economic warfare is not confined to wartime situations. When the Cold War had become a settled reality as a result of mutual fears, suspicions, and recriminations, the United States government began, in 1947, to develop the notion of an embargo policy against the USSR and other Communist states.[15] Although motivations were mixed, ranging from a sheer desire to express righteous antagonism to the idea of waging comprehensive economic warfare against the Communist "bloc," the main purpose came to be that of maintaining Soviet, and later also Chinese, military inferiority, presumably in the interest of curbing their appetites for aggression. This was to be achieved by an export embargo on so-called "strategic" goods in two categories: first, military equipment and, second, civilian goods that would serve to increase the economic base of Communist, especially Soviet, military strength. The intent was to weaken, not to coerce.

Since Communist states would be able to import most of the goods in question from other industrial states, the problem of implementation was to make these latter join in the embargo. In the late 1940's, the United States used its economic power to impose the policy on its reluctant allies by threatening to cut off economic and military aid to them at a time when American economic aid to the West European countries was several times larger than the total turnover of their trade with the Communist states of Eastern Europe. This economic pressure was eventually formalized in the Battle Act of 1951 by which the President was authorized to cut aid to any uncooperative aid recipients if he deemed this step to be in the national interest. No cutback or elimination of aid ever occurred. At the time, the threat was effective to the extent that pressure was needed. To coordinate Western policy for purposes of the embargo, two committees were established, the ministerial Consultative Group, which was to give policy guidance, and the permanent Coordinating Committee (COCOM) to draw up the embargo lists. Following the outbreak of the Korean War, a more restrictive export embargo was placed on trade with China. The difference, called the "China differential," was made up of certain types of goods allowed to be shipped to other Communist countries. This embargo passed the General Assembly of the UN in May 1951. CHINCOM, the China Committee, was set up in 1952 to administer the embargo. The members of the coordinating committees were the members of NATO (except for Iceland) and Japan.

The embargoes certainly cut back trade. United States exports to the Soviet "bloc" plunged from $397 million in 1948 to $145 million in 1949, and $41 million in 1950, that is, by nearly 90 per cent. Exports by the West European states shrank from $792 million in 1949 to $268 million in 1950, or by about 60 per cent. China's trade with non-Communist countries decreased from $1170 million in 1950 to $601 million in 1952, or by almost one-half, but expanded again to $1,113 million in 1956.[16]

A crucial question in designing and evaluating such a policy concerns the meaning of "strategic goods." Military systems, such as warships, tanks, and guided missiles create no problem of identification and, particularly in the age of nuclear deterrence, the merit of an embargo on weapons exports is not much complicated by the consideration that a military industrial capacity

enlarged by steady exports is a potential advantage when a war
of attrition rises. It is an embargo on "civilian" goods adding to
military economic potential which poses complex problems. Two
concepts of such "strategic goods" have been evolved. The cruder
one simply requires someone in authority to make the judgment
that such things as locomotives and steel-making equipment are
"strategic goods." The more sophisticated concept recognizes that
the restriction of trade involves economic costs to the restricting
state as well, and therefore that goods should be embargoed only
if there is a "*net* strategic advantage" in doing so. But this concept
does not solve the refractory problem of identification. Any fairly
developed economy of the size of the Soviet economy around 1950
can of course allocate and combine productive resources in order
to produce national outputs of varying composition and, mar-
ginally, varying size. From a strictly economic point of view,
whether such a country is better off by importing, say, military
aircraft and producing food or textiles at home, or by doing the
opposite, is a matter of comparative production efficiency, including economies of scale. Past Soviet governments were determined
in any case not to depend on foreign supplies of military, or indeed any essential, goods as a matter of strong political preference.
But the choice of substituting the production of one thing for
that of another, and to rely on imports for satisfying complementary needs exists on many levels and in many output areas. The
import of typewriters and toys releases labor for the armament
industries, assuming, of course, that resources have been set
aside for the production of exports. From the economic point
of view, the decisive criterion turns on the differences, in the
importing state, between the ratios of domestic production
costs and the price ratios of goods that could be imported. Since
good information about such ratios, in any case subject to change
over time, is virtually impossible to procure about Communist
national economies, the selection of goods for the embargo list
with a view to reducing an opponent country's economic military potential on the microlevel faces insuperable difficulties.
There is an exception to this in the case of items of high technol-

ogy in which, for a time, domestic production is unable to substitute for imported products. In the 1960's, advanced computers were an example of this kind of product. There are, however, macroeffects that can be aimed at. If the foreign trade of the target state is substantially reduced by means of an embargo, over-all productivity is lowered. This might have a retarding effect on the country's industrial and military development unless it proves possible to make the private consumer shoulder the entire burden of the shortfall in aggregate labor productivity.

Such consequences depend naturally on the effectiveness with which an export embargo is implemented. From the beginning, some businessmen in Western Europe found ways to circumvent the COCOM regulations and were helped in doing so by a less than zealous attitude of their governments. From 1954 on, the allies of the United States pressed hard for progressive relaxations. The COCOM lists were revised and, by 1958, included only items which were understood conventionally to have indubious "strategic" importance. The British government decided unilaterally, after unsatisfactory negotiations with the United States, to abolish the "China differential" and to apply the less inclusive COCOM list to trade with China. All other Western European governments followed suit immediately. By 1970, the United States itself began seriously to review the embargo policy, and in the following year, Congress passed legislation aimed at increasing trade with the Communist countries (excluding North Vietnam), and authorized the Export-Import Bank to supply credits toward this end. The 1971 announcements of forthcoming visits by the President to Peking and Moscow expressed the abandonment of the patterns of confrontation which had characterized the Cold War.

Lack of data preclude even an approximate estimate of the effects of the embargo on the economic and military development of the Soviet Union and China. An over-all conclusion is nevertheless feasible. To begin with, it may be granted that the embargo imposed some cost on the Soviet economy. In certain lines of production, the Soviet Union was compelled to achieve self-sufficiency more quickly than the Soviet striving for autonomy in essential products demanded in view of immediate costs to overall production. However, during the 1960's, the Soviet Union managed an average rate of economic and industrial growth which was one of the highest in the world, and considerably exceeded that of the United States. The embargo certainly had no crippling effect. At best it might have prevented the Soviet economy from developing still faster. Nor is there any evidence that the Soviet military sector suffered. The fact is that Soviet military strength grew relatively to American military strength over the decade. At its end, the Soviet Union had achieved approximate parity with the United States in strategic nuclear capabilities, and had gained on the United States in general-purpose forces by a steady expansion of the Soviet navy. This conclusion is shared by Ota Sik, a knowledgeable top Czech economic planner who went into exile after the Soviet occupation of Czechoslovakia in 1968. Testifying before a Senate Committee, he said: ". . . no hindrances to and limitations of East-West relations, such as embargoes and similar measures, can prevent the growth of Soviet military power. On the contrary, this embargo policy only contributed to Soviet efforts to render autonomous various militarily important sectors of production, quite apart from the fact that a large country rich in natural resources always finds means to prepare all important products and supplies from outside, even in the face of the strictest embargo policy." [17]

It is possible that China's economic and military development was affected somewhat more than the Soviet Union's, particularly after the USSR cut her trade with China to a trickle. But the overwhelming influences on Chinese industrial development were the inscrutable gyrations of government policy (e.g. the "Great Leap Forward" and the "Cultural Revolution"). There is no clear-cut evidence that China's economic and military development was in any way crippled, or even seriously held back, by the embargo.[18]

Against any small and uncertain gains must be set the heavy costs of the embargo. First, by restricting trade with the Communist countries, the United States and its allies were foregoing any gains in economic productivity which foreign trade confers. Second, the maze of regulations and controls made the trade of the embargoing countries less efficient than it would have been otherwise. Third, the American pressure on its allies caused incessant frictions and squabbles, and the inevitable resentments could only weaken the cohesion between these allied states. Fourth, the Soviet Union became probably somewhat more self-sufficient as a result of the embargo than would have been the case otherwise. Fifth, the policy had the side effect of increasing the political and economic hold of the Soviet government over the East European Communist countries. Sixth, the embargo may have strengthened the domestic power Stalin wielded in the Soviet Union.[19] Seventh, the embargo acted as a persistent irritant in East-West relationships even when a *détente* was regarded as desirable in the West. While the embargo was meant to weaken an antagonist, it also helped to reinforce his antagonistic posture. As Alexander Eckstein put it with reference to the China embargo, if one distinguishes between a state's *capacity* for aggression and its *propensity* for aggression, an effective export embargo may diminish the capacity while stimulating the propensity for aggression.[20] Eighth, the enforcement of the embargo involved substantial administrative costs in the United States and among its allies. Although all these costs can no more be quantified than any uncertain gains, it is impossible to suppress the judgment that the United States embargo policy was on balance very costly to the United States.[21] It was an expensive mistake.

Given this experience, one may also infer that even a comprehensive and technically efficient embargo on exports, though it can hurt a large and developed national economy, cannot produce a critical impairment. The circumstances under which an embargo could be made comprehensive in terms of goods (i.e. a flat embargo on *all* exports) and in terms of exporting countries (i.e. an embargo on all sources of imports) are unimaginable. Once there are holes in the embargo, futility is a foregone conclusion. This conclusion may not be true for a small and underdeveloped country, but who needs an embargo to reduce the military development of a small and poor state?

Trade Restrictions as Power Plays in Time of Peace.   As stated, the purpose of economic measures employed as power plays is either to threaten or execute economic punishment in order to coerce or to weaken another economy for noncoercive reasons. Coercive use always implies an offer to cease the punishing action on condition of compliance with the coercing government's demands. Usually, therefore, coercive employment follows and is accompanied by verbal communication. However, this is not always the case, at least openly; and it is, therefore, not clear in a number of historical cases whether trade restrictions or embargoes are designed to influence or to weaken the target state. The Soviet Union, in particular, has preferred implicit threats in its economic power plays. Not rarely, one suspects, the unstated purpose of imposing punitive measures was to deter third states from following the example set by the punished actor. And in some cases, punishment may have served mainly to satisfy the emotional needs of the punishing government.

In the following, we will ignore fairly routine exercises of market power. There is discrimination of sorts, real or apparent, whenever public or private traders do not import supplies at the lowest available prices, or export to customers making the highest bids. Such discrimination may occur inadvertently because market knowledge is imperfect,[22] or be deliberate because a stable market or supply is worth something overtime. When import quotas and foreign-exchange control are employed, perfect nondiscrimination is hard to achieve even if intended. But we will likewise disregard deliberate attempts to manipulate the terms of trade by restricting exports and/or imports, as long as these attempts are modest. In any case, these possibilities arise only when suitable price elasticities of demand and supply generate an appreciable degree of monopolist or monopsonist market power. Besides, to fix on optimum rates of restriction is extraordinarily difficult in view of limited market knowledge, and attempted gains may also prove illusory when other countries retaliate.[23] In any case, these tricks of commercial policy are examined in textbooks on international trade theory and policy.[24]

We will first briefly describe two cases of economic warfare, and then refer to additional ones in the subsequent analysis. Following Khrushchev's accession to power and his attempt at reconciliation with Yugoslavia, Soviet interest in Albania lessened perceptibly, and the uneasy Albanian leaders began to explore expanded relationship with the West and particularly China. After the Hungarian revolution, when the rift between Moscow and Belgrade widened once more, the Albanian government felt temporarily reassured. But in 1959, Khrushchev again promoted a rapprochement with Yugoslavia. Moscow's relations with Albania became less close and deteriorated rapidly because of Soviet displeasure with the growing amity between China and Albania. At a conference of Communist states in Bucharest in June 1960, Albania openly backed Peking against Moscow. Little and very poor Albania was highly dependent economically on the USSR and hence vulnerable to economic pressure. In 1959, the year before Moscow exerted economic power, 56 per cent of Albania's imports came from the Soviet Union (followed by 12 per cent from Czechoslovakia and 8 per cent from East Germany); 45 per cent of her export went to the USSR (19 per cent to Czechoslovakia, 14 per cent to East Germany, and 7 per cent to Hungary). Moreover, while Albania's imports consisted primarily of essential food and industrial goods critical to her economic development plans (e.g. tractors, trucks, machinery), her chief exports to the Soviet Union were cigarettes and tobacco (45 per cent). In addition, Albania's economic development had become very dependent on Soviet loans.

Soviet pressure began in March 1960. The Soviet Union delayed trade negotiations with Albania and cut back on loans and technical assistance. Soviet statements make it clear that Moscow hoped for a split in the Communist leadership in Albania and a return to the fold. In a Sino-Albanian agreement of April 1961, China obligated herself to lend Albania a credit of $123 million for industrial development. Five days later, the Soviet Union canceled all aid to Albania. Soviet exports began to slacken. Diplomatic relations were broken off in December, and by the end of 1961, all trade relations had come to an end. Albania was also expelled from the Soviet-led Council of Mutual Economic Assistance (COMECON), but the Soviet government did not press the East European Communist states to sever their economic relations with Albania completely. Their trade with Albania did, however, drop in 1962. The results are clear. Albania suffered acute economic distress. She had to cut back her industrialization program, especially since Chinese deliveries were slow. Albanian leaders expanded their country's ties with the capitalist world. Despite her economic problems, the Albanian government preferred independence to economic comfort.[25]

When Fidel Castro seized power in Cuba in 1959, the island's economy had been extremely dependent on the United States ever since Cuba gained political independence. American businessmen had made huge investments in her latifundian agriculture, mining, banking, and tourist facilities, totaling $1 billion. In 1958, 67 per cent of Cuban exports went to the United States, and 70 per cent of her imports originated there. Most of the equipment in the island's industries was from the United States. Under the Costigan Act of 1934, the United States bought the bulk of Cuban sugar exports at an artificial price substantially above world market prices. In 1958, the bonus resulting from this preferential treatment alone amounted to about $150 million.

Although the Cuban leader castigated the United States throughout 1959 and early 1960, vituperatively denouncing her as an aggressive imperialist, Washington remained restrained in its initial responses. In February 1960, the Soviet Union and Cuba concluded a barter deal involving Soviet oil and Cuban sugar. In March, President Eisenhower asked Congress for stand-by authority to cut sugar imports from Cuba. Early in the summer, Cuba seized the oil refineries owned by Standard Oil of New Jersey and Texaco because they refused to refine Soviet crude oil. Shortly afterwards, Washington terminated all remaining aid programs to Cuba. In July, it canceled all sugar purchases for the

balance of the year. A month later, Castro retaliated by nationalizing United States property valued at half a billion dollars. In
October 1960, the United States imposed an embargo on all
exports to Cuba except for food and medicine. Diplomatic relations were ruptured in January 1961, after extensive economic
agreements had been concluded between Cuba and the USSR in
December 1960.

The United States then proceeded to push other trading countries to curtail shipments to Cuba. The Foreign Aid Act of 1963 included a clause requiring the President to stop aid to recipients
who refused to restrict shipments to Cuba unless he found it in
the national interest to waive the penalty. When a British firm
sold 450 passenger buses and a French concern, a number of locomotives to Cuba, the United States government invoked the Act,
to the pointed displeasure of the nations involved, but found its
leverage negligible since remaining aid programs to the two allied
countries were in any case approaching the vanishing point.
Spain and Morocco were more vulnerable and accepted satisfactory compromises. In the case of fourteen other countries, the
President used the waiver. The United States also sought to tighten
the economic boycott of Cuba through the Organization of
American States (OAS) on the ground that the Cuban government engaged in revolutionary propaganda and subversion in
most of Latin America. In January 1962, the OAS voted, against
six abstentions, to expel Cuba from the organization; and in July
1964, the OAS decided with fifteen votes against four to sever
diplomatic and commercial relations with Cuba. Mexico refused
to cooperate from the beginning. When Chile acquired a new
government in 1970, with a strong Communist participation under
Señor Allende, she resumed diplomatic and economic relations
with Cuba.

Regarding results, there is no question that Cuba suffered economically from the United States embargo. Unavailable spare
parts lowered the efficiency of much of her capital equipment. The
boycott of Cuban sugar had no effect to the extent that United
States sugar imports from other exporting countries opened up

markets previously supplied by them. But the loss of premium income resulting from the United States preference clearly hurt. The United States probably succeeded if it simply wanted to punish Cuba, although Cuba may have been able to transfer a part of the bite to the Soviet Union, which committed itself to her support. Yet the United States wanted to achieve more than that. Secretary of State Dean Rusk announced four objectives of the embargo:

To reduce Castro's will and ability to export subversion and violence to other American states; to make plain to the people of Cuba that Castro's regime cannot serve their interests; to demonstrate to the peoples of the American Republics that communism has no future in the Western Hemisphere; and to increase the cost to the Soviets of maintaining a Communist output in the Western Hemisphere.[26]

United States policy certainly succeeded in the last objective. Success in the other three appears doubtful. And there is no question but that this policy failed to topple the Castro government or to make it more amenable to the wishes of the United States. It may well be that Cuba's economy would have utterly collapsed under the embargo if she had been isolated. But the fact is that the Soviet Union and other Communist as well as non-Communist countries came to her help or traded with her. If this was a burden to the Soviet Union, as it surely must have been, its government is likely to have derived commensurate satisfaction from besting the United States in "her backyard." And the cost to the United States, aside from the loss of investments and the value of Cuban trade, minus the sugar bounty, was a considerable loss of respect and goodwill in Western Europe and the underdeveloped world, including much Latin-American public opinion. As an exercise in economic warfare, United States policy hardly rates as a success.[27]

Other interesting cases since World War II is the Arab boycott, begun in 1955, of companies owning business properties in Israel; and the Soviet use of trade reprisals against Yugoslavia (begun in 1948, and again in 1957), Australia (1954), Finland

(1959), and China (1959–1960).[28] (Over this period, membership in the General Agreement on Tariffs and Trade of 1947 [GATT] has normally precluded the use of trade sanctions by the major capitalist nations.)

Scrutiny of a large number of cases reveals that this sort of exercise of national economic power has been only rarely successful, even though the reduction or elimination of trade was usually accompanied by complementary pressures involving credit, economic aid, and technical assistance.

This observation requires two immediate qualifications. First, measures through which pressure has been exerted recently are still continuing in several of the recent cases, and the results as of now may not be conclusive. But regarding the Arab boycott, Sino-Soviet relations, Soviet-Albanian relations, and the United States-Cuban rupture, it is nearly unimaginable that the results are not definitive. The target actors have found viable ways of accommodating themselves. The Arab boycott was never more than a matter of pinpricks. The Soviet Union and China have recently agreed to expand their trade. Albania's trade with the COMECON countries is considerable, and her rift with Moscow has become much less articulate. The United States embargo against Cuba could possibly still succeed only if the Soviet Union were to cut its trade with, and aid to, Cuba—an extremely improbable event.

The second demurrer hinges on the precise purpose for which the economic measures were undertaken. They failed to coerce. But it is not always wholly clear that the purpose was purely coercion, especially in several of the instances involving the Soviet government, which usually did not make its threats, and the purpose of its measures, explicit on the level of public communication. The self-image it projects on this level is that of the good actor grievously wronged. As has been noted, an actor who does feel betrayed or otherwise wronged, may simply want to lash out in anger and get emotional satisfaction from punishing the other party. Or he may have wanted to demonstrate firmness to third states.

Our cases point clearly to the two principal factors that account for the usual failure of trade reprisals to coerce. First, no matter how apparently dependent the target country is on the trade with the state attempting an economic power play, the government under pressure can usually turn its eliminated trade gradually to other partners and/or get other support from third countries. In 1948 and 1956, Yugoslavia turned to increased trade with non-Communist states; and in 1954, when the USSR—as the result of a dispute over a Soviet deserter—switched her large wool purchases from Australia to South Africa, it was easy for Australia to sell her wool to countries previously supplied by South Africa. Third countries are normally ready in time of formal peace to play this accommodating part for one or both of two reasons. For one, trade with the target of economic pressure may simply be profitable if only because prices are attractive. For another, one third state or more may be political opponents of the state exerting pressure and will seize the opportunity to weaken the latter diplomatically. To the target state this means considerable relief from pressure it has been exposed to. Such relief, to be sure, may be slow in coming, though it need not be. The target state will inevitably suffer transient economic distress. The adverse blow will take some time to take economic effect since this kind of economic warfare employs sanctions that cannot work quickly, but rather are attritional. There is likely to be economic distress once the effects accumulate and before expanded trade with other states comes to the rescue. However, and this leads to the second reason for the usually successful resistance to economic power plays, a suffering economy is not dead or moribund. The hurt is not unbearable as long as there is political determination to defy economic pressure. Whatever the burden, it is less than what societies often put up with in time of war. Belts may have to be tightened, but nobody is killed or maimed. If defiance of economic pressure is courting military conflict, the economic power play is only part of a more complex and dangerous game. The threat situation is then decidedly different.

Resistance to foreign economic pressure, then, is in part a function of the strength of government. As long as governments are firmly legitimate, undivided, and enjoying strong domestic support, this other basis for successful noncompliance prevails. Two factors tend to promote national unity in the face of this kind of international crisis. The very assumption by the power-exerting government that one would buckle under to economic pressure is, at least in the modern world, sensed as insulting, and yielding would be registered as demeaning and ignominious. This attitude is widespread because of the second factor, namely the now almost universal sway of nationalism which makes societies keenly sensitive to international affront. As long, then, as international economic and political competition makes the monopolist and monopsonist market power of some states over others very precarious and subject to swift dissipation, and as long as pressured governments are resolute and domestically strong, the prospects for economic warriors are bound to be dim.

On the other hand, to wage economic warfare is costly. The disruption of trade involved will necessarily involve some economic costs to the state wielding economic power unless, and to the extent that, trade had been subsidized, as was the case with the sugar bounty that Cuba received from the United States. In free-enterprise countries with relatively democratic regimes, the firms and interest groups on which these costs fall, in the first place, are apt to press for compensation or for cessation of the policy concerned. Indeed, in such societies governments will usually be reluctant to seek international leverage by these means. The frequency with which the Soviet Union appears in our case material may well in part reflect the fact that its government has been in a strong position to impose the burden of economic warfare upon the population.

This sort of economic power policy is likely to entail other costs as well. Especially if it is a matter, more frequent than not, of a big trading country employing it against a much smaller one (e.g. Soviet Union versus Yugoslavia and Albania, the United States versus Cuba), the spectacle of bullying is likely to evoke a critical response in many third countries. This may happen even in allied countries, particularly if these are pressed to participate in the exercise of economic power. Neither the United States nor the USSR has escaped this censure. Moreover, if the target state resists, its adaptive response will ordinarily strengthen it and decrease the degree of putative economic power that the power-wielding state enjoyed before the event. Furthermore, government and public in the target state will, at least for some time, bear grudges if not positive hostility to their would-be oppressor. There will be a scar effect. Also, the considerable risk of failure is itself an inherent cost. The "big bully" looks foolish when he is defied successfully. His prestige is involved. His putative economic power has been revealed to be hollow for this sort of economic warfare. Finally, the state making the economic power play may be violating the rules or spirit of international or regional norms to which it has previously subscribed. Thus, the General Agreement on Tariffs and Trade (GATT) is designed to preclude or at least minimize international commercial discrimination. And the Charter of the OAS provides that "no state may use or encourage the use of coercive measures of an economic or political character in order to force the sovereign will of another state and obtain from it advantages of any kind."

Countries differ in two general ways regarding their ability to wage and resist the kind of economic warfare under discussion in this section. One general way in which they do *not* differ in this respect is an appreciable gap in economic development between contending states, except to the extent that it affects difference in "size," to be discussed shortly. The cases involving Albania, China (PRC), and Cuba indicate that a comparatively low state of development does not preclude resistance to economic pressure provided the two crucial elements—the will to resist and the ability to expand relations with third states—are given.

Size is a relevant factor of general import. Economic warfare in time of formal peace is ordinarily for big powers against small countries, or anyhow for big trading states against lesser ones, volume of trade being the critical dimension of magnitude in these matters. The size difference is normally critical because a marked degree of monopolist and monopsonist market power is a prerequisite, at least for rational decision-making, to the initiation of the economic power play. And, subject to structural factors, size of trade favors market power. The bigger trading country exploits an asymmetrical relationship of interdependence.

The relevant difference in "size" can be increased, of course, if the state wielding economic power is joined by friendly or allied countries in imposing the economic sanction. In the Cuban case, we saw that the United States attempted, with no more than partial success, to persuade the members of the OAS, and to persuade or coerce countries receiving aid from the United States, to participate in the embargo. In the cases of Yugoslavia, Albania and China, the Soviet Union was joined to varying degrees by its fellow members in COMECON. For waging economic warfare, co-operation by COMECON members is important because the Soviet Union is, despite her geographic and population size, a far smaller trading country than the United States or Japan. Since about two-thirds of her trade is with other members of the Communist camp,[29] she has more over-all market power there than in the non-Communist world,[30] although she can, of course, increase the trade dependence of particular "smaller" countries by cultivating trade with them. In terms of the "size" requirement, the members of the European Economic Community, especially if joined by the United Kingdom, will certainly acquire the world's largest *economic* basis of economic power. Accounting for 40 per cent of world exports and only a somewhat smaller proportion of world imports, the EEC will rank first, ahead of the United States and Japan. Whether the EEC countries will be politically inclined, and united enough, to use this economic capability as a political instrument—in other words, provide the other basis of economic power—is a different question.

The other general factor which generally favors the exercise of economic power relates to the political and economic regime of states, and particularly to the manner in which foreign trade is carried on. In the highly developed capitalist countries of the West, diffused economic and political structures do not as such afford a favorable institutional framework for waging economic warfare by means of manipulating foreign trade flows. As history demonstrates, it can be done, but it takes great governmental effort and presupposes a high degree of political unity and determination. The institutional framework is far more favorable in countries that practice state trading, exclusively or predominantly. Present-day Yugoslavia excepted, the Communist states are exceedingly well equipped from this point of view. In the Soviet Union, for example, the Foreign Ministry has the foreign-trade monopoly. It buys exports from Soviet exporters and sells imports to Soviet importers. It does the bargaining and is therefore in direct command of whatever monopoly or monopsony power the country may enjoy vis-à-vis others.[31] Within the usual constraints of assuring essential imports and roughly balancing exports and imports overall, it can switch trade at the government's discretion. It can do so, moreover, without any announcements, so that, if an economic power play is launched, the target state receives no advance notice unless there have been preceding threats, whereas governments in capitalist democratic states usually require extended public debate before such a policy is approved.[32] And, finally, authoritarian Communist governments are in an excellent position to impose on their population whatever economic costs may accrue. In fact, true price relationships are so obscure in socialist command economics that the extent of the burden and its distribution could not be matters of public, if indeed of government, knowledge.

From an institutional point of view, then, the big state-trading country is well set up to conduct economic warfare against small countries. What is the record? There is considerable evidence that the Soviet Union exploited other Communist countries between the end of World War II and 1953–1954 by rigging the relative prices of imports and exports as well as by exacting reparation deliveries (from Communist governments whose countries had been on the German side during the war) and by the use of joint-stock companies.[33] Yet, to the extent this was true, it resulted presumably more from political and military than from market power. In any case, the only way to discover systematic attempts at exploiting market power through state trading is by comparing the terms of trade between states and groups of countries. Such comparison has not yielded conclusive evidence of the deliberate use of market power by Communist state-trading countries since the mid-1950's. When contracts are negotiated with market economies, world market prices are normally employed; and if the exports of Communist state-trading states are, not infrequently, overpriced, a compensatory overpricing of import prices can be usually observed. In fixing export and import prices among themselves, Communist authorities commonly use the prices in the (capitalist) world market.[34]

We do not know why the Soviet Union has made sparing use of its institutional advantage for practicing economic warfare against non-Communist countries, and why China has not done so vis-à-vis her neighbors. One expert surmises that Marxist philosophy inhibits such exploitative practice ideologically.[35] This may well be true, especially since Marxists see in these practices one of the characteristic evils of capitalism. Yet like all ideological restraints, this one does not always work, especially between Communist antagonists; ideologies have a way of weakening over time. There is also the fact, previously noted, that even the Soviet Union has not in the past generated a volume of trade with non-Communist countries large enough to afford much monopolist or monopsonist market power.

The conditions of economic warfare through trade sanctions indicate the measures small trading countries could adopt in order to reduce the risk.[36] They are: (1) to distribute their foreign trade over many countries differing in political alignments; (2) to keep their exports competitive and diversified and push exports encountering favorable demand elasticities abroad; (3) to avoid high dependence on vital imports for which the foreign sources of supply are very concentrated; (4) to maintain as "rounded" an economy as possible; (5) to decline preferential trade agreements with individual states; (6) to support an international trading system prescribing trade discrimination; and (7) to prac-

tice a conciliatory diplomacy. Needless to stress, the pursuit of the
first five of these safety measures can be costly economically,
and the pursuit of the last can be costly in terms of political
preferences.

Collective Economic Sanctions

Both the League of Nations and the United Nations Charters provided for collective economic sanctions meant to coerce a militarily
aggressive state into a cessation of hostilities, or a state violating
some other norm into conforming behavior. In principle, collective
trade sanctions should be more effective than economic reprisals by
one state or a few, since they would be based on an internationally
cumulative degree of monopolist and monopsonist control over
the world market. The situation of the target country would be
extremely difficult, if not untenable, if its requirements for imports were vital and *all other* states participated in the sanctions.

In practice, however, collective trade and other economic
sanctions have proved abortive. In the League case against Italy's
attack on Ethiopia (1935–1936), insufficient international compliance made the deprivation inflicted in Italy too mild to prove
decisive. By a UN resolution of December 1966, economic sanctions have been applied against Rhodesia, anathema to large UN
majorities on account of her repressive domestic policies toward
her black population. In this instance, too, the wall of trade
sanctions has proved leaky. There are always traders who find
evasion profitable. Neighboring Zambia determinedly reduced her
trade with Rhodesia, but her economy was too closely intermeshed
with the latter's to permit all commerce to be cut off at once.
Above all, South Africa and Portugal continued to support Rhodesia heavily. There is no doubt that the Rhodesian economy has
suffered serious harm. Her large tobacco industry was virtually
crippled and her agriculture generally was hurt by the inability to

import ammonia for fertilizer production. Economic growth was stifled, and inflation became strong. Yet, by the beginning of 1972, the Rhodesian economy was functioning, and its government viable. Whether this condition will continue to prevail indefinitely remains a question. But it appears that even widely applied economic sanctions are clearly not effective enough to bring quick, if any, results as long as an actual blockade and punishment for noncompliance are absent from enforcement.[37]

The reasons for the ineffectiveness of collective economic sanctions are clear.[38] First, some states are apt not to share, or even oppose, the goal on behalf of which economic reprisals are applied. They may even identify politically with the target state. Second, the economic as well as the political costs of imposing sanctions may be very high to some country or countries which carried on a large volume of trade with the target state, usually as a result of geographic propinquity (e.g. neighboring Zambia vis-à-vis Rhodesia). Third, the authorities in free-enterprise countries may find it difficult to stop illicit trading. Fourth, as long as the government of the target state enjoys strong domestic support for the policy which led to sanctions against it, the effect of coercive measures is often to increase rather than diminish political cohesion in the target society.[39] Of course, coercion may not be the only purpose of collective sanctions. To the extent that the object is to signify international disapproval or the emotional gratification derived from a punitive act, even relatively ineffective sanctions may prove worth while. However, if compliance is to be enforced, the probability of success is very low.

The Foreign Trade "Carrot"

In view of the difficulty of deriving political leverage from using the stick of trade reprisals, what are the conditions of obtaining it from offering the carrot of special trade benefits? Surprisingly, the historical record does not show this means of international coercion to have been practiced much in recent decades. Nazi Germany did so toward Hungary and Rumania before World War II. Since that war, however, such cases have been rare, or else they are not matters of public record, or have failed to receive attention. Inattention and lack of publicity could result from the fact that the tendering of the carrot is not commonly regarded as plainly coercive as the brandishing of the stick. Dangling the carrot can be made to look like inviting a *quid-pro-quo* bargain; and it is in practice often difficult to draw the dividing line between the one and the other. In principle, of course, coercion does take place whenever the economically weaker party feels compelled to undertake a reciprocal action he is loath to perform. Yet since he is presumably free formally to take the carrot or leave it, the pressure involved in a promised reward is less objectionable and arouses less hostility than in a threatened penalty.

Since nearly all countries with market-type economies are members of GATT, they are obligated not to offer tariff preferences that they are unprepared to generalize to other countries. When these states want to offer economic rewards, they usually do so by offering loans or economic aid. Some of them, to be sure, give certain commercial preferences to particular other countries. Thus, Great Britain has been giving preferential access to her market to West Indian sugar and New Zealand butter. France is maintaining preferential arrangements with a number of her former colonies in sub-Saharan Africa. The United States is giving preferred access to its market to sugar from the Philippines. Yet these are institutional residues of enduring historical relationships which, in most instances, originated in a previous status of colonial or other formal dependency. To the extent that these special economic ties persist, they characterize now a patron-client relationship; and it is doubtful that their continuation lends itself to exerting economic pressure in the contemporary world. The EEC has recently extended preferential trade agreements to several less developed Mediterranean countries, and in March 1971, unilaterally reduced tariff duties on certain manufactured and semimanufactured exports of ninety-one, that is to say, all less developed countries—a volume of trade estimated at $1 billion.[40] And the United States has declared its readiness to make similar concessions. These are unilateral concessions involving no *quid pro quo*. They have been made in response to the persistent demands of the less developed countries for support of their economic development in this form.

The reasons that give state-trading states an institutional advantage in waging economic war by trade reprisals also greatly facilitate the adroit use of the economic carrot. Their governments need not induce private traders to pay higher prices for imports or to accept imports of poorer quality. They can simply do it, and do it without verbal fuss. An example of such practices is the Soviet wooing of Iceland in the 1950's.[41] The Icelanders, in the majority basically neutralist, had resented the British occupation in 1940, and felt the United States military base established during the war, and still in existence, to be a nuisance, even though Iceland became a member of NATO. In the early 1950's, Iceland had a series of quarrels with Great Britain concerning fisheries, Iceland's main export industry. When Britain established an embargo on Icelandish fish in retaliation against Iceland's extension of her territorial waters from three to four miles, the Soviet Union stepped in, in 1953, and bought Icelandish fish chiefly in exchange for oil. Although there was no formal Soviet demand for political concessions, Iceland proceeded to force some diminution of her defense treaty with the United States in 1954. By 1955, the Soviet Union had become Iceland's top trading partner. However, as a result of Icelandish indignation about the Soviet crushing of the Hungarian uprising in 1956, Iceland's relation with the USSR cooled, and her government changed its position about the maintenance of the NATO base on her territory. There have probably been other instances in which the Soviet Union made favorable trade offers, not to coerce by holding out reward for compliance with express conditions, but rather in the hope that helpful trade offers would in time elicit a rewarding political response.

Then there is the Soviet readiness to come to Cuba's aid in February 1960, when the United States had proclaimed its embargo. Indeed, the Soviet agreement to purchase the bulk of Cuba's sugar crop may have involved price concessions amounting to an admixture of Soviet aid. Here again, the Soviet interest had nothing to do with coercion by offering a reward: the essence of the action was to support the viability of a regime which, though perhaps of doubtful Communist maturity, opposed the United States, and opened an opportunity for the USSR to gain significant influence in an area supposedly in the United States sphere of influence.

On the basis of available evidence, it is unclear to what extent the Soviet Union has employed the promise of commercial favors to gain political ends by this form of coercion. Trade advantages have been used, probably a great deal, in the *hope* of securing influence in other countries. Sometimes, no doubt, these hopes came true. For this purpose, the ability of socialist state-trading states to make long-term contracts has been some advantage unavailable to governments in charge of market-type economies. However, this advantage turned out necessarily to be less persuasive over time than it seemed at first. The experience is that long-term contracts do not really stabilize trade substantially. As practiced by the USSR and other Communist states, the long-term contract is not binding. Beyond the first year, it requires annual renegotiation.[42] This requirement would facilitate economic power plays, whether by means of the stick or the carrot. But, as has already been observed, Soviet practice does not suggest eagerness to indulge in economic power plays one way or the other. The Soviet government, it seems, is first of all concerned, when organizing foreign trade, to serve pragmatically its own economic needs for imports. Like the capitalist nations, it has preferred the means of credit and economic aid for the purpose of supporting clients and aspiring to political gains.

Notes

1. Walter L. Levy, "Oil Power," *Foreign Affairs*, 49 (July 1971): 652–655.

2. Robert Owen Freedman, *Economic Warfare in the Communist Bloc* (New York: Praeger, 1970), chap. II.

3. Cf. Paul Y. Hammond, *The Cold War Years: American Foreign Policy since 1945* (New York: Harcourt Brace, 1969), p. 89.

4. *The New York Times* (January 8, 1972), p. 10.

5. Jacob Viner, *International Economics* (Glencoe, Ill.: Free Press, 1951), p. 346.

6. Wiles, *Communist International Economists*, pp. 478–480. For numerous historical examples, see Eugene Staley, *War and the Private Investor* (New York: Doubleday, 1935).

7. Hirschman, *National Power and the Structure of Foreign Trade*, p. 53; Edward Mason, *Controlling World Trade* (New York: McGraw Hill, 1946), p. 98.

8. Quoted in Marshall I. Goldman, *Soviet Foreign Aid* (New York: Praeger, 1967), p. 14.

9. *The New York Times* (September 13, 1970), p. 5.

10. *The New York Times* (June 8, 1970), p. 1; *The Christian Science Monitor* (April 17, 1970), p. 1.

11. *The New York Times* (January 9, 1972), p. 1.

12. *Ibid.* (December 3, 1971), p. 1.

13. These policies and techniques are fully described and analyzed in the classic book on the subject: Yuan-Li Wu, *Economic Warfare* (New York: Prentice-Hall, 1952). The reader is referred to it for detail.

14. Wiles, *Communist International Economics*, pp. 465–466.

15. This section is chiefly based on the best treatment of the subject: Gunnar Adler-Karlsson, *Western Economic Warfare, 1947–1967* (Stockholm: Almquist & Wiksell, 1968).

16. A. Doak Barnett, *Communist China and Asia* (New York: Harper, 1960), p. 233.

17. *The New York Times* (December 9, 1970), p. 23.

18. This is the conclusion of Alexander Eckstein, *Communist China's Economic Growth and Foreign Trade* (New York: McGraw Hill, 1966), pp. 264–265.

19. Ota Sik, referred to above, testified that the embargo helped "the reactionary, Stalinist, forces." *The New York Times* (December 9, 1970), p. 23.

20. Eckstein, *Communist China's Economic Growth*, p. 269.

21. This is the conclusion of the Swedish analyst on whose careful work this section is largely based. Adler-Karlsson, *Western Economic Warfare*, p. 10.

22. Wiles, *Communist International Economics*, pp. 223–224.

23. Cf. J. E. Meade, *Trade and Welfare* (New York: Oxford University Press, 1955), Vol. II, chap. 17; Kindleberger, *Power and Money,* p. 127.

24. See also Gardner Patterson, *Discrimination in International Trade; the Policy Issues: 1945–1965* (Princeton: Princeton University Press, 1966).

25. Freedman, *Economic Warfare in the Communist Bloc,* chap. III.

26. Quoted in Adler-Karlsson, *Western Economic Warfare,* p. 210.

27. The description and analysis in this section have been based largely on Adler-Karlsson, *Western Economic Warfare,* chap. 17.

28. On the Soviet cases see Freedman, *Economic Warfare in the Communist Bloc,* chaps. II–IV; Wiles, *Communist International Economics,* pp. 499–513.

29. *The New York Times* (March 24, 1971), p. 15.

30. Wiles, *Communist International Economics,* p. 414.

31. *Ibid.,* pp. 30–33, 41, 158–160.

32. *Ibid.,* pp. 476–477.

33. Marshall I. Goldman, *Soviet Foreign Aid* (New York: Praeger, 1967), chap. I.

34. Wiles, *Communist International Economics,* pp. 40, 219, 238–244, 498–499.

35. Wiles, *ibid.,* p. 499.

36. For a similar list, see Wiles, *ibid.,* p. 20.

37. Robert McKinnell, "Sanctions and the Rhodesian Economy," *Journal of Modern African Studies,* 7 (1969): pp. 559–581.

38. See the best treatment of collective sanctions: Margaret P. Doxey, *Economic Sanctions and International Enforcement* (London: Oxford University Press, 1971), pp. 138–139.

39. Cf. Johan Galtung, "On the Effects of International Economic Sanctions, with Examples from the Case of Rhodesia," *World Politics,* 19 (1966), pp. 378–416.

40. *The New York Times* (March 31, 1971), p. 1.

41. Wiles, *Communist International Economics,* pp. 517–518.

42. Wiles, *ibid.,* pp. 416–417.

CHAPTER

7

The Uses of Economic Power (II)

Economic and Military Aid

The present chapter continues the analysis begun in the preceding one. Its focus is primarily on the derivation of national economic power from the extension of economic aid and technical assistance, including military assistance.

Economic or financial aid given by one government to another is not a novel phenomenon. It has been practiced among sovereigns throughout history. In Europe, during the seventeenth, eighteenth, and early nineteenth centuries, for example, England and France in particular often paid "subsidies" in order to cement alliances or support allies, especially those whose geographic separation rendered direct military aid impractical.[1] In the nineteenth century, loans took the place of subsidies. The United States Lend-Lease Act was a modern version of the traditional subsidy.

But interstate economic aid, extended in time of peace, did not assume a massive scale until after World War II. It would be surprising if there were any state at the present time which had not recently given or received such aid. The United States was the first big donor to appear on the international scene. It began with the Marshall Plan, aimed at meeting the postwar reconstruction needs of the West European nations and, after 1950—the year when the Korean War started—was expanded to cover an increasing number of recipients in the economically underdeveloped world. The Soviet Union, which at first had denounced all Western aid, economic or military, as a technique for establishing or maintaining control or predominant influence over the recipient states, commenced her own career as a big donor in 1955. China (PRC) began succoring neighboring Communist countries in 1953 and non-Communist states in 1956.[2] Indeed, large-scale economic aid originated primarily as a function in the Cold War between the United States and its allies and the Communist states. Even the Marshall Plan was largely justified by the need to restore economic health to the West European countries and thereby to render them resistant to Communist subversion from within. With the Truman Doctrine, American aid was given at first outside Europe for bolstering feeble allies facing, or believed to face, Communist pressure, and then was extended to less developed nonallies as a means of containing Communism. Beginning in the middle 1950's, both the USSR and the United States were using economic aid in a competitive effort to obtain and support client states.

However, although Cold War rivalry stimulated a larger flow of economic aid than would have emerged in its absence, relatively wealthy states, not primarily or at all engaged in the East-West conflict, adopted the practice and, through the United Nations and its specialized agencies, a substantial amount of aid has been channeled multilaterally. Nor is it only rich states which have been giving aid to poor ones. Poor countries have also given economic aid, usually with political objectives clearly apparent. Thus, China —with one of the lowest incomes per capita—gave $212 million of aid in the 1960's to socialist South Yemen, North Korea, and other states.[3] Though she gave little in 1968 and 1969, when preoccupied with internal problems, China obligated herself to a spectacular $709 million in 1970 as compared with $204 million from the USSR.[4] India has extended aid to Nepal and Sikkim. She financed completely two successive economic development plans in Sikkim (1954–1961, 1961–1966). In 1966, incidentally, Sikkim's per capita income was estimated at double the Indian.[5]

This has been a typical patron-client relationship, based on a shared suspicion of China. Saudi Arabia, Kuwait, and Libya, not poor but underdeveloped, gave considerable financial assistance to Jordan and Egypt after the war with Israel in 1967.[6]

FOREIGN AID: DEFINITION AND PURPOSES

Foreign economic aid is defined as a concessionary transfer of resources from one government to another. It can take the form of goods (e.g. steel-mill equipment or food) or of financial funds that represent a claim on real resources. Foreign aid is thus distinguished from other international flows of resources, such as trade or private foreign investment, which are based on market incentives rather than concessionary terms and often do not involve governments as actors. Governments can supply aid as a gift (or grant) or as loans. In the case of gifts, the assets of the donor decline by the same amount that those of the recipient increase. Loans would not constitute aid, by our definition, if they were made strictly as a business investment in order to earn interest. There is a real transfer of resources only to the extent that the nominal amount lent exceeds the present discounted value of interest and amortization payments. When a loan is made as a financial investment, the lender will avoid such an excess and attempt to do better. But many loans between governments contain a substantial, though variable, grant element. For instance, a loan may be extended free of interest, or with a low interest rate (e.g. often lower than those prevailing in the donor country), or with interest only to commence after a number of years. Not rarely, interest payments may be deferred subsequently and, occasionally, interest and even principal may be forgiven altogether. Such loans are often called "soft." Loans represent aid, in other words, precisely to the extent that funds are priced on concessionary terms. On the other hand, certain conditions of gifts or loans reduce the grant element. This is true when loans are "tied," that is, required to be spent on the purchase of goods in the donor country or be shipped in vessels belonging to the donor state. The amount by which the price of imports is increased thereby constitutes a subsidy (a grant) to the export and shipping industries of the donor state. The amount involved reduces the grant element to the recipient.

Technical assistance is a special form of international aid. It constitutes a transfer of technological expertise on a concessionary basis. If paid for by aid funds, which are not outright gifts, it is only partially a grant. In the following, it will be treated as economic aid except for certain special characteristics that will be noted when relevant.

Military aid, as practiced between governments, takes the forms of special technical assistance (e.g. military training) and/or supplies of military equipment as a gift or on credit. The grant element is again a variable. Sometimes the straight sale of military equipment involves a special kind of concession when it involves items that are not normally for sale. Again, military aid will be treated as economic aid in most of the following analysis.

It is not easy to get at the true purposes for which economic aid is given. Among the rationales that have appeared with any frequency, genuine philanthropy or humanitarianism is only one, and, it is generally assumed in the literature,[7] merely a small fraction of foreign economic aid can be safely attributed to a plain sense of human solidarity or to a sincere feeling that the wealthy, among nations as well as within them, have the responsibility to help and share with the destitute two-thirds of mankind. All other, clearly self-regarding rationales, can be classified, as follows, in terms of short-term and longer-term objectives:

1. Expected Short-Term Economic Payoffs
   a. To stimulate additional commercial exports.
   b. To get rid of burdensome surpluses (e.g. agricultural products, obsolete military supplies).
   c. To stimulate the foreign production of raw materials for importation.
   d. To stimulate or preserve abroad a favorable attitude toward foreign private investment, or to promote the development of public overhead capital that encourages such investment.
2. Expected Short-Term Political or Military Payoffs
   a. To compete for political influence in the donor country against

rival states, i.e. to curb or to displace their influence or to protect one's own influence; also to gain or keep military allies or to disrupt antagonistic alliances.

b. More basically than (a.), to gain or preserve the friendship of the donor state.

c. To consolidate the position of a government or regime which is subject to economic pressure, or to domestic or foreign political pressure, but whose preservation is politically or militarily favorable.

d. To enhance the military security of the donor state.

e. To project internationally the image of a country which cares about world poverty.

f. To signal to third states a political commitment to the recipient country.

3. Longer-Term Payoffs: The immediate rationale here is to support economic development in the recipient state, helping it break out of the vicious circle of perpetual poverty and proceed to a process of self-sustaining economic growth. But, except to the extent that pure philanthropy is operating, ultimate benefits are expected from the economic development of recipient states. Some of the listed short-term payoffs reappear as long-term benefits. Thus:

a. As poor countries become economically more developed, they will offer richer export markets and more attractive fields for foreign private investment.

b. Similarly, as the economic capacity of poor countries steadily improves, their governments and regimes become more secure domestically, and their own capability to resist external aggression is enhanced.

In addition, however, long-term expectations also involve benefits in terms of the entire international system, of which the presently poor countries are so large a part, at least in numbers of independent states and in numbers of population. Thus:

c. As poor countries become better off economically, their behavior will become less disruptive and cantankerous, and more stable and peaceful.

d. The economic growth of the destitute countries is also expected to produce a more congenial world environment in terms of institutions and policies. In the United States, for example, it has often been assumed that economic development promotes pluralistic or "democratic" government, and free economic enterprise; and this is regarded as a boon either because of pride in one's own institutions, or because it is believed to be easier to get along with societies organized like one's own.

Although this list contains the most frequently encountered rationales for extending foreign aid, it is not complete. There are also the special aid relationship existing between some ex-imperial countries and ex-colonies. For instance, France gives a great deal of aid to several of her former African dependencies, and one is hard put to find anything but vague reasons given for the maintenance of these enduring patron-client relationships. It may very well be that some influential Frenchmen still earn income from investments previously made, or profit from preferential access to these markets.[8] Yet these material gains are puny compared with the large volume of aid; and, as in Chad, any French economic stake is virtually nonexistent in some of the countries.[9] There may also be some desire to maintain French influence and cultural ties, and a lingering sense of *mission civilatrice*. And beyond such self-interest, there is the desire "to defend the system established by the colonial power on granting independence . . ."[10] Hence, a feeling of responsibility and perhaps, less avowable, feelings of pride and guilt may be present. The protégé relationship grown out of a previous colonial or semicolonial connection has also affected the aid activities of Great Britain, Belgium, the United States (i.e. the Philippines), and Australia (vis-à-vis Papua-New Guinea).

It is also clear that a substantial volume of economic aid is given at any one time simply because it has been done before. Bureaucratic inertia (and self-interest) keeps it going without a more than perfunctory review of the erstwhile reasons that led to its inception. Finally, we disregard here so-called "aid" which is given and received strictly as a *quid pro quo,* as a payment for something specific that is bought by means of aid, whether it is an air base or a vote on an issue in the UN. There is no real grant element involved in such cases. Aid is here simply a disguise for a purchase price or a bribe, a fact understood by both parties.

The reasons publicly advanced for seeking or accepting foreign aid are likewise varied. The familiar official rationale, probably operative in many instances, is that additional resources are needed for national economic development or defense. In poor as in wealthy states, the actual top priority of governments is usually to stay in office, and to do so as comfortably as circumstances permit; and getting control over additional resources can help in many ways, even if not in terms of promoting economic growth. To seek relief from a painful deficit in external accounts may be a rationale. Or the symbolic act of commitment by the donor state may be treasured for its international security implications. On the recipient side, too, the motivations are apt to be multiple, and official reasons for seeking or taking aid will not necessarily coincide with the operating objectives.

It is easy to see that, under propitious circumstances, aid given without any strings whatever, or with strings regarded as legitimate by recipient and donor alike, may lead to influence by the donor state because the recipient identifies positively with the donor, not because he feels he owes something to the donor. The result is then an interdependence of fully compatible preference functions. The achievement of influence is, in that event, noncoercive. Nor is there anything mysterious about military or economic aid functioning as sheer support of a government, regime or country by increasing the recipient's economic or military capabilities, or about the withdrawal of such aid weakening a country. But aid as an instrument of coercion, or functioning as coercion, is less easily understood.

It will be readily agreed that any threat to cut off economic aid, unless certain conditions are met, is coercive, and so is any termination of aid accompanied by statements that its resumption depends on the recipient's behavior in certain respects. Of course, economic aid may be terminated for other reasons. The recipient may no longer require it; the donor, pressed financially, sloughs off aid programs of marginal importance to him; the recipient has joined an alliance regarded as hostile; etc. An attempt at coercion is involved only when both parties understand that the former recipient must do something specific in order to effect a resumption of aid. Whether the offer and delivery of aid—a positive sanction as defined in Chapter 1—contains a coercive element is a more difficult question to which we will now turn.

Coercion enters whenever the recipient's choices of behavior are restricted by the conditions of the grant; that is to say, if he is obligated to co-operate with the donor for mutual benefit. If co-operation is a condition of the grant and comes forth only as a result of the condition, it is not freely given; it does not issue from a shared genuine spirit of co-operation. Aid is noncoercive only if there is unconstrained unity of purpose in the aid transaction between donor and recipient.[11] Aid given for some advantage to be received by the donor is a "pseudo gift." [12]

It is of course true that, though conditions attached to aid offers are in themselves coercive by restricting the choices open to the recipient, the receipt of economic resources enriches his choices in another direction. A recipient government will presumably not accept aid unless it values the expected choice-enriching effects more than the restriction of choice implicit in aid conditions. But if the two effects balance one another off in the recipient's evaluation, he will not feel *aided*. The transaction is a *quid pro quo*. Hence aid is a "pseudo gift" in such cases. The recipient will then participate in the language of aid only because such participation is another condition of receiving aid. And he may feel coerced if the imposition of unwelcome conditions makes him feel that his economic weakness has been taken advantage of (which an act of *aid* would preclude); and he may suspect further that by accepting aid, and becoming dependent on it, he becomes vulnerable to future demands.

It is possible that no obvious string is attached to aid, and that the donor has no intention to coerce, or is unaware of any coercive effect his conditions may generate, yet the recipient nonetheless feels coerced. Coercion has a subjective as well as an objective aspect in an ambiguous aid relationship. The two parties know that they are not equals in capability. Aid will increase their interdependence but the initial and resulting degree of dependence is asymmetrical. The recipient is usually weaker or poorer and needier than the donor. The recipient is and may feel dependent on receiving aid, whereas the donor is not dependent, or nearly as dependent, on giving it. After all, in extreme cases, the recipient becomes a subservient client of the donor.

In most instances, the donor pursues an instrumental purpose in granting aid. He is using the recipient instrumentally. Even if the donor state gives aid for the immediate and exclusive purpose of fostering the economic progress of the aid-receiving state, he is likely to lay down conditions. He may do so only because any government transferring public funds abroad wants to, or must, assure its public that these moneys are being used for acceptable development objectives and that none are siphoned off through corruption or being condemned to waste through inefficiency.[13] What economists in the donor country are wont to demand as the only "string," is that programs for using aid be negotiated in order to assure their effectiveness as a means to economic progress.[14] This preoccupation with effectiveness has often led to insistence on program aid rather than project funds, the former requiring the employment of aid as an integral part of an over-all economic, monetary, and fiscal plan, designed to bring economic growth about. As Albert Hirschman has trenchantly observed, virtue is then being imposed coercively. Having one's arm twisted in such a manner, however noble the intent, is not like a consumer buying a bicycle. Such conditions on receiving aid amount essentially to a "semi-colonial situation." [15] Especially, program support looks "imperialistic," since it involves prying into the internal affairs of the recipient.

If we grant the presence of a coercive element in many international aid transactions, we do so on the understanding, however, that the level or weight of coercive pressure is a variable. Even the threat to cut off aid unless certain conditions are met tends to be less coercive than the threat of war which involves massive destruction of life and economic assets rather than the mere withholding of economic resources, however desirable their receipt might be. Furthermore, to threaten an economic penalty is on a higher coercive level than the promise of a reward. And the coercive content in the promise of reward will vary with the nature of the conditions attached to it. They can be more or less severe, i.e. costly, to the prospective recipient, the costs touching on various values—economic, political, and psychological. This means

also that the coercive level is not only an objective matter in the
sense of a particular promise being of equal positive and negative
value to any number of recipients. As we have observed above,
there is clearly a substantial subjective factor since the sensitivity
of prospective recipients is dictated by the specific structure of
their values.

With the coercive content of aid a variable, at the extreme of
the lower end there are offers of aid, or of the continuation of aid,
which will be void of any coercive element when the recipient is
expected to do things which he prefers to do, or toward which he
is completely indifferent. In either case, no price is exacted, or it
may happen conceivably when no conditions whatever have been
laid down by the donor state. But in view of the checkered history
of past aid relationships and their frequent manipulation by donor
countries, the recipient government may disbelieve the avowal of
altruism and regard supposedly unconditional aid with suspicion of
hidden motives, and with the apprehension that, by accepting such
aid, it is setting itself up for blackmail later. It is for this reason
that prospective recipient governments have not rarely rejected gifts
and preferred the explicit setting forth of reciprocal obligations.
In the 1950's, for instance, Morocco insisted on receiving loans
rather than pure grants from the United States, even though the
grant was to be tied to United States military base rights. India
has repeatedly preferred the reciprocal nature of loans when the
United States was willing to make a gift.[16] Not seldom the recipient
wants to know the full price of aid.

TYPES OF INSTRUMENTAL PURPOSE

Three principal types of instrumental purpose can be distinguished when governments use aid in order to actualize national
economic power. First, coercive cutoffs or the threat thereof;
second, aid used to gain or retain influence over the donor state;
third, aid given to support a donor state, government, or regime;
and fourth—reflecting other rationales—aid extended with the
expectation of affecting the role of the underdeveloped countries
as a group in the international political and economic system.

Two problems, inherent in this classification, must be understood in advance. While spectacular cases of threats to terminate aid or of actual termination acquire enough notoriety to receive widespread attention, the threat as a mere hint, one assumes, usually takes place in private, and is ambiguously inferential when made in public. The hint may not be outwardly coercive, but is meant and understood to be just the same. Available case material is therefore unrepresentative of resorts to the vague threat. To give an example, after Egyptian President Sadat had ousted several prominent pro-Soviet leaders from his cabinet, Soviet President Podgorny in a newspaper interview in May 1970, while on a visit to Egypt, "pointedly recalled that Soviet assistance to Egypt in the last ten years had totalled $720 million," and that Soviet aid contributions for the next five years were scheduled at $500 million.[17] The other problem concerns the distinction between aid extended in order to obtain influence and aid given to support the recipient. While there are a few cases which belong in one category or the other, in most instances by far the two aims are pursued simultaneously and their pursuit becomes inseparable. For example, military aid may be granted to support the military strength of a government or state subjected to external or internal threat or pressure. Yet it can also be given in order to secure influence, especially over the military, in the donor country. We will, first, present briefly a few examples in each category and then analyze the effectiveness of the aid instrument for each kind of purpose.

Coercive Aid Cutoffs. 1. In December 1948, when the Netherlands government was recalcitrant about granting independence to Indonesia, the United States threatened to withhold Marshall aid, and in fact some aid shipments were suspended subsequently. Two months after the cutoff, the Dutch government resumed negotiation with the Indonesian Republic.[18]

2. In 1948, and again in 1958, the Soviet government terminated economic aid to, as well as trade with, Yugoslavia. Yugoslavia did not yield.

3. In 1952, Secretary of State Dulles threatened "an agonizing reappraisal" of American commitments to Europe if the projected

(supranational) European Defense Community were not ratified
by the nations involved. The Senate added pressure by discussing
the possible denial of mutual security funds. But in August 1952,
the French National Assembly rejected the treaty.

4. When the Sino-Soviet rift grew serious in 1960, the first
economic reprisal was the recall of Soviet personnel engaged in
technical assistance. Economic pressure was ineffective, if pressure
was intended, to make the Chinese leadership more co-operative.

Economic Aid for Influence. 1. The achievement of influence
can be safely assumed to be an aim of a great power in alliances
with small and poor countries which they support by means of
military and economic aid as well as by treaty commitments.
Thus, in 1969, the United States maintained "mutual defense"
treaties with forty-five countries, most of them small and poor,
and receiving aid from the United States. To the extent that the
governments of these countries felt their external military security
to depend on American aid (e.g. South Korea, South Vietnam,
Cambodia, and Israel in 1970–1971), and to the extent that governments perceived such dependence regarding their domestic viability,
their political autonomy was subject to curtailment, and the United
States was exercising influence whenever such curtailment actually
occurred. It is reasonable to assume that the autonomy of such
governments as those of Cuba and Egypt was subject to similar
jeopardy as a result of their dependence on the Soviet Union.

2. Like the United States, the Soviet Union has used foreign aid
on a broad scale. She has used aid in smaller Communist countries
where it competed for influence with China (e.g. North Vietnam,
North Korea, Mongolia).[19] Involved in great-power competition
for influence with the United States, the Soviet government has
given aid to countries which were unfriendly to the United States
(e.g. Cuba and several Arab countries), which were unaligned in
the Cold War confrontation (e.g. India and, at times, Indonesia),
and which were aligned with the United States (e.g. Iran and
Turkey). A case of overwhelming economic support is Afghanistan,[20] which received about $700 million worth of aid from 1954
to 1959.

3. An example of a firm patron-client relationship gone sour is Pakistan. Through most of the 1950's and the early 1960's Pakistan was known as a stanch ally of the United States. The latter gave her more than $4 billion in aid and largely equipped the Pakistan armed forces. While the United States counted on Pakistan as an ally against the Soviet Union, Pakistan's governments were persistently concerned with their tense relation with India. When war between these two countries erupted in 1965, the United States embargoed arms shipments to Pakistan, and its government turned to the Soviet Union, China, and Britain for additional arms. Thereafter, Pakistan increasingly cultivated close relations with China.

4. In 1955, the Soviet Union surprised the world by concluding a spectacular arms deal with Egypt, which made the latter henceforth independent of Western sources of supply. In 1956, the United States, disturbed by the rising solidarity between Moscow and Cairo, withdrew a tentative offer to finance the huge Aswan High Dam project. President Nasser retaliated by nationalizing the Suez Canal Company. The ensuing military intervention by Britain and France, in conjunction with Israel's, came to naught in the face of United States and Soviet disapproval and threats. With Soviet diplomatic and economic backing, the Arab states shook off Western dominance in the region. Total Soviet economic aid to Egypt alone came to $1,011 million from 1954 to 1969, and other Communist countries contributed another $562 million (Syria and Iraq received a total of $443 million and $432 million, respectively, from the two sources).[21] After the Israeli-Arab War, the USSR poured an enormous amount of military equipment and assistance into the area. There is evidence that when the USSR started her huge aid program in the Middle East, her leaders hoped not only to reduce or displace the influence of the United States and Britain but also to gain political leverage for influencing the *internal* political development of the Arab states.[22] But such influence never materialized, especially not in Egypt where domestic Communists were outlawed and persecuted.[23] There is no doubt that increasing dependence of Egypt gave Moscow con-

siderable influence. But it seems to be an influence of dubious
scope, depth, and duration, while having been costly economically
and also having drawn the Soviet Union into a militarily dangerous
entanglement.[24]

Aid to Support Government, Regime, Country. As noted previously, donor actions to build up a position of influence over, and
to support, a weak government, regime, or country, are in most
instances inseparable exercises of national economic power. The
support function is usually more conspicuous in the extension of
military aid, though, as noted, such aid also lends itself to attempts
at obtaining political influence. It is also true that the line between
economic and military aid is, especially functionally, arbitrary,
since the receipt of economic aid may release local resources for
a military build-up, since the receipt of military aid may set free
resources for investment, and since particular aid projects financed
under either rubric—for instance, the construction of highways or
railroads or port facilities—may serve both purposes. Nevertheless,
it is arguable that Soviet and Chinese support of North Vietnam in
its war against the United States, and United States support of
South Korea, were intended primarily to effect support.

1. From 1946 to 1968, the United States gave $38.8 billion in
military aid, compared with $94.7 billion in economic aid.[25] Fol-
lowing World War II, the United States launched the Marshall
Plan to restore the economic viability of the dislocated national
economics of Western Europe and also of Japan. This gigantic
support action was clearly meant to bolster the strength of the
recipient countries against the Communist "peril." Later, the large
Military Assistance Program (providing more than $10 billion
through 1954) and security guarantees were added in order to
provide strength against any external military threats.

2. The most important and expensive support operations of the
USSR involved China until 1960, several Arab states and India
since 1956, Cuba since 1959, and North Vietnam since the early
1960's. Thus, China received substantial credits after the outbreak
of the Korean War and the imposition of the export embargo by the

United States and its allies. Total Soviet credits have been estimated at over $1,300 million.[26] Among other things the Soviet Union delivered 166 complete industrial plants during the first Chinese five-year plan ending in 1957, and committed herself to 125 more plants in aid of the second five-year plan (1958–1962). In addition, China received numerous patents and blueprints. About 10,800 Soviet and 1,500 East European technicians were sent to China between 1950 and 1960; and 8,000 Chinese skilled workers and engineers and 7,000 Chinese students were sent to the Soviet Union.[27] Beyond doubt, this was a huge transfer of resources in support of China's industrialization; and China received military aid as well.

Total Soviet *military* aid given from 1955 to 1970 has been estimated at $19 billion, of which $12.7 billion went to other Communist states.[28] At first, the Soviet government was reluctant to give such aid to non-Communist countries. Only ten such countries received aid in 1962. Yet, twenty-five non-Communist states received Soviet military aid in 1970.[29] American aid was on a similar scale but went to more numerous recipients, and hence was less concentrated.[30]

AID LESSONS

The following analysis will consider, first, some specific problems associated with the threat of terminating aid, the use of aid for building positions of influence, and the use of aid for supporting the capabilities of particular countries or governments. Second, we will examine further problems germane to all three purposes.

1. The historical record does not establish the termination of aid, or the threat to suspend it, as a generally effective measure of international coercion. The degree of effectiveness, to be sure, is often hard to measure, especially when desired results express themselves only with a considerable delay. Jacob J. Kaplan may be right in his surmise that the termination of American aid to Indonesia and Ghana "undoubtedly contributed to disillusionment with Sukarno and to the downfall of Nkrumah." [31] The trouble

is that other factors usually operate in the same direction and that we have insufficient knowledge to attribute comparative weight to them. Thus, whether the suspension of arms shipments to Pakistan and India brought about a cease fire or contributed much to it is impossible to say. Certainly the vigorous role of mediator assumed by the USSR was important in this respect. Examination of a large number of cases suggests a failure to coerce by this means. Aside from a few cases involving rather trivial matters, the only successful one involving United States pressure are the above-mentioned action against the Netherlands in 1948, and that on all of its allies, in connection with the embargo policy against Communist states, until 1953 or 1954. The reason for these favorable outcomes is immediately apparent and points to one major, if not predominant, condition of the more common failure. Until 1953, when Western European nations had not yet recovered fully from the ravages of World War II, and the world dollar shortage was still acute, they had simply no alternative donors to turn to. By the mid-1950's, the economic recovery of the developed allies of the United States had progressed enough to make them less dependent on American aid. For many of the poor countries receiving aid, dependence on the United States decreased in 1956 when the Soviet Union became an alternative source of economic and military aid. All the spectacular failures on record can be attributed in large part to international rivalry, and the consequent ability of pressured governments to seek relief from other states. The coercive use of aid is in this respect like all attempts at economic coercion. Putative economic power is the harder to actualize, the keener is the competition between economic powers. It follows that aid-dependent countries are the safer from the whip of the aid stick, the more they cultivate or exercise the option of taking assistance from rivaling donors.

However, while the conspicuous brandishing of the aid stick is not often blessed by desired results, it does not follow that the putative economic power inherent in the donor's position also tends to be ineffective when the relationship between two parties is untroubled, or less troubled. Assessing the empirical facts is unfortunately very difficult in these undramatic cases. But it is easy to imagine that donor officials make frequent hints in private to recipient officials indicating some difficulty in the assurance of a continued flow of aid if certain conditions are not met. The suggestion may not always be taken, but the point is surely that a vague, inferential and seemingly helpful hint about possible difficulties at the source of funds, made at times when smooth relations prevail, is less offensive, if offense is registered at all, than are explicit demands made in the limelight of publicity, and as part of a deteriorating relationship in which hostile feelings have been already aroused.[32] Once a crisis has erupted and pushed noneconomic stakes, including the values of prestige, honor, and autonomy into the foreground, only utter dependence will permit economic coercion to become effective. The widespread fear of "neocolonization" among actual and potential recipients of aid makes submission to the open threat of economic deprivation too costly and hence improbable. If the veiled and muted threat without fanfare is apt to be most effective, we may also conclude that, in many instances, the recipient will anticipate some of the donor's wishes and prefer, at no overt cost to self-respect whatever, to satisfy them quietly before an issue has arisen, or before even a hint has been given.

If the open and explicit attempt to coerce a recipient by terminating, or threatening to terminate, aid is very low in terms of probable effectiveness, it tends to be also inefficient because the costs of failure are likely to be appreciable. While failure does not receive attention when a suggestion is made and goes unheeded, the salience of the open power play insures failure costs dearly in the international prestige of the donor state and the domestic reputation of its government; and in this especially, as so many cases, the recipient turns to an international rival for relief. On top of the humiliation of an abortive threat, the previous investment in aid can then be written off. Indeed, given the historical record, one is tempted to wonder whether coercion by means of aid cuts in any but exceptionally favorable circumstances can ever be the rational objective of government. Whatever the words used by the donor, perhaps the desire simply to hurt is uppermost, even if it is usually the kind of punishment that pains the punisher more than his target.

2. Regarding the use of economic aid as a means to acquire or defend positions of influence, it should be understood that it is not international friendship which is at issue. Friendship—which is anyhow rare between societies—is a matter of diffuse esteem, respect, and affection which prospers best among equals. A persistent donor-client relationship, characterized by sharp differences in power and wealth, is bound to inhibit feelings of friendship. International friendship, previously established and rooted in other conditions, may survive the donor-recipient relationship, if handled with care on both sides; it can hardly be created by economic aid in time of peace.

When foreign aid is used for promoting influence in a cold war environment fashioned by two rival great powers, four types of donor-recipient relationships are conceivable: [33] first, the recipient genuinely identifies itself with the benefactor and becomes a voluntary ally; second, the recipient comes to dislike the donor and turns neutralist or joins the opponent; third, the recipient becomes completely dependent on the donor's aid, loses much or all of his autonomy, and ends up as a satellite; and fourth, the recipient, though substantially dependent on the donor's aid, retains considerable autonomy and becomes a conditional ally. However, too many variable factors are involved in these outcomes to permit the design of an analytical model attributing different results to particular combinations of inputs. Specific personalities and specific combinations of circumstances are often involved.[34] Nevertheless, some generalizations are possible.

Aid tends to be most effective in producing influence when it is cementing a formal and solid alliance. In that case, it is harder for the recipient to maximize his autonomy by preserving or cultivating the option of resisting pressure from the powerful ally by means of going over, or threatening to defect, to the side of his opponent. To be sure, nominal allies have not seldom quit and followed the highest bid. But such mobility presupposed that perceived security needs did not stand in the way.

The aid-for-influence game is clearly much harder to play when the target countries have alternatives, and particularly when they can play one big power off against the other. Indeed, in view of the historical record since World War II, the very conditions of mutual antagonism that made the big donor states seek to establish influence, or reduce the opponent's influence, tend to make the game expensive and positions of influence precarious. The more competition, the less do the competitors tend to get, and the more they bid up the price. In fact, the postwar record is hardly calculated to cause elation in either superpower. The Soviet Union has lost all or some influence in other Communist states (e.g. China, Yugoslavia, Albania, and Rumania), an effect surely regretted by Soviet leaders who have regarded Moscow as the natural capital of the world Communist movement. Indonesia has proved fickle to all sides. The present influence of the USSR over several Arab states is obviously dependent on the absence of an enduring settlement with Israel. Its greatest success is perhaps in India where, however, influence must be exercised with great reserve. Despite a huge volume of aid, the United States has fallen far in terms of world influence from the zenith reached immediately after World War II. Aid to many of the Arab countries could not in the end assure influence. The relationship with Pakistan has gone sour, and those with India, Iran, and Turkey have cooled. Latin-American countries have become increasingly eager and able over the past dozen years to assert strenuously a jealous aloofness to United States policies.

In addition to the competition for influence between the two superpowers, there has been another major factor, representing an apparently secular trend, which has diminished the prospect of purchasing influence cheaply by means of aid. The price has risen, the yield has diminished. There is, on the most general level, the waxing hold of international norms, fully displayed in caucuses of the United Nations, which flatly denies the legitimacy of situations of international inequality; and a position of unilateral influence spells lack of equality. There is furthermore the luxuriance of nationalist sensitivity in the economically less developed world which has been subservient to great-power dominance in the past, as in Latin America, or has experienced the misery-making conditions of colonial dependence. As Uri Ra'anan has cogently observed, the pride and touchiness of African and Asian leaders disposes them to overreact to great-power demands. Indeed, defiance of great powers gives these leaders great appeal to their followers; and material considerations, even aspiration of economic growth, are of secondary importance compared with the need to submit, or the appearance of submission, to great-power influence, including that of donors of aid. These widespread and, if anything, growing attitudes can only reduce the political leverage of economic and military aid. It is no longer rare that economic power turns out hollow when exercised, and that the donor ends up appeasing the recipient whose sensitivity has been irritated.[35]

These general conclusions about the utility of economic and military aid as an instrument of establishing a donor's position of influence over a recipient do not mean that this instrument has become useless in the contemporary world. They merely mean that the price tends to be high and achieved influence fragile, and not likely to endure for long. The prospects are naturally better where special circumstances are favorable, e.g. when the client strongly depends on the patron for military security as well as economic bounty, or when the client identifies squarely with the patron for reasons of ideological, racial, or cultural affinity. Needless to stress, the chances of success are improved also by the client's exercise of diplomatic skill and of tact. Tactfulness rests on understanding the recipient's need for the respect due to a sovereign actor, for his need of basic autonomy, and must weigh the recipient's disagreement with the donor on certain matters. This amounts to saying that, in this era of world politics, effective influence presupposes the admission of a degree of counterinfluence. But tact and empathy are not central to the nature of bureaucracies involved in foreign policy and aid, and they are particularly hard to produce and sustain if patron and client differ greatly in political and economic ideology as well as in power and wealth.

3. Compared with the uses of aid for purposes of building a position of influence or of attempting coercion, its use for supporting a weak country, government, and regime seems to have been fairly effective, at least from a superficial perspective. To be sure, the American attempt to shore up the fumbling nationalist regime in China in her struggle with Mao's forces was foredoomed to failure, and, at the beginning of 1972, the United States seemed to face the same experience in Indo-China. Resources of the kind that can be supplied from external sources cannot render viable a feeble regime confronted by a determined and resourceful domestic foe. Yet the economically developed countries whose recovery from the devastations of World War II was helped so generously by the United States (i.e. Western Europe and Japan) have for the most part done extremely well; and very few of the many less developed states that have received American aid have gone under as a result of internal turmoil, or have been subjected to successful foreign aggression. This holds true also of the Soviet Union's client states.

There are two important considerations, however, which require this verdict to be discounted appreciably. First, it simply cannot be demonstrated that most of the many states supported by the United States were ever in real danger of external aggression or internal collapse abetted by external machinations. They would certainly have been less well off materially without American aid, but they might well have survived and achieved increased viability on their own. For example, the Soviet Union was perhaps actually deterred from invading or putting severe military pressure on Western European states by the commitments of the United States. Yet, it is possible that Soviet governments were deterred by other considerations or never recognized any interest in an aggressive policy toward Western Europe. South Korea and Taiwan excepted, similar reflections are not out of place regarding Asia. Hypothetical history, of course, does not carry much conviction, and courts a sarcastic response when taken too seriously. Yet the point needed to be made that much support of other countries was premised on hypothetical contingencies.

The second consideration concerns the identity of the government or regime supported by economic or military aid. The problem is that this identity is apt to change over a period of time. A government or regime may draw support when it fits the donor's conception of a favorable world environment in terms of its economic system or political complexion, because the recipient supports the donor's regional or global policies at the time, or because it seems susceptible to being influenced by the donor, etc. As some donor states have experienced, however, these bases for giving support may quickly disappear in this extremely dynamic world. How much value does the Soviet Union derive now from the support it once extended to China and Yugoslavia; and how much future value will it derive from the help now granted to several Arab countries and Cuba? Similarly, how much comfort does the United States receive now from the economic and military support given to many Latin-American states?

4. All three purposes of using economic and military aid raise some general questions. Central among these are the costs of aid to the donor and recipient countries.

While financial disbursements on account of foreign economic and military aid have been very large since World War II, it is far from easy to get a correct picture of net financial outlays. Not all foreign aid announced is actually drawn upon. This holds true especially of Communist donors who offer aid agreements covering several years. And eventual net payments are much smaller if loans are serviced in terms of interest and amortization.[36] However, the immediate resource outlays have been substantial. One factor tending to make outlays large is the "quicksand" effect. Once aid has been given to the donor, it is hard not to continue doing so. This entrapment effect can be resisted, but not without determination and the willingness to accept the recipient's displeasure. The economic opportunity cost to the donor societies is naturally the alternative uses, public or private, that have been foregone. Finance expended on aid is unavailable for outlays on defense, welfare, or private consumption. To the extent the donor country taxes itself on account of aid outlays, and convertible currencies are involved, no pressure is put on the balance-of-payments even if recipient *B* buys exports from third country *C,* which in turn imports from donor *A.* In addition, foreign aid imposes substantial administrative costs, as is evident from the swelling ranks of embassy staff, military missions, and bureaucracies at home.

Then there are various intangible costs incurred at home and abroad. The public may be politically divided about foreign aid generally or about aiding particular recipients, and government authorities are apt to suffer a consequent loss of support for other activities. For instance, American military aid as a whole aroused strong opposition when the official military posture of the United States came under increasing domestic attack on account of the intervention in Vietnam. This problem points to the question of exactly to whom domestically aid-giving is costly. If the extension of aid is looked at as the production of public good, the distribution of the costs depends upon the structure of the tax system (or on the differential impact of inflation if aid is not financed through tax revenues or borrowing). In any case, some who are compelled to pay, care little or do not care at all about the public good for which they pay and which they are free to consume. And the same situation obtains with reference to political and moral costs. Since bilateral aid relationships exhibit some tendency to corrupt both donor and recipient, among these moral costs may be an undue inflation of righteous and supercilious self-importance or, as Senator Fulbright put it, an "arrogance of power." Some people enjoy the arrogance, others despise it.

In addition, there are the risks of becoming entangled in regional squabbles abroad. This happened to the United States when it was censured by both India and Pakistan for having lent assistance to the other. In fact, extending aid to some countries will not rarely provoke the hostility of others. China, for instance, regarded Soviet military aid to India as provocative, and similarly assumed

American aid to India to be motivated by an anti-Chinese animus.[37]
Moreover, military aid extended by A to B (who is afraid of C)
may induce the latter (who may be afraid of B) to increase his
military strength, possibly by accepting aid from another great
power. Support has then been nullified. Such a result may be
satisfactory if the establishment of influence over B is the object
of A's aid. But it is unsatisfactory, if the object is to support B.

However, if there are many contingencies which tend to diminish, if not obviate, the over-all effectiveness of foreign aid, account
must also be taken of the fact that, in a world in which many
countries give aid, refraining from doing so may entail costs as
well. As the United States has experienced on several occasions
when it refused to extend military assistance involving expensive
aircraft to poor countries on the ground that they were not needed
for security reasons, and that their acquisition would be at the
expense of economic growth, the rejected governments turned to
France or Russia from which they promptly received the desired
equipment. As Charles Kindleberger remarked, while giving aid
may not gain good will, withholding aid will lose it.[38] And is it
possible for a big and affluent society in the contemporary world
not to lose international prestige if it abstains from granting aid
altogether?

Officials and literature in donor countries are strikingly less
sophisticated about the various costs of *receiving* aid. Yet apprecia-
tion of these costs is a prerequisite to understanding why giving
aid fails so often to achieve the donor's objectives. We have
explained above the difference between loan and grant, and the
grant-reducing effect of various restrictions (e.g. tied loans) which
donor countries often attach to aid. A reminder of the long-run
impact of aid given in the form of loans is the rapidly snowballing
public indebtedness of the recipient countries. The Pearson Report
estimated the total at $50 billion by the end of the 1960's, and
growing at an explosive 17 per cent a year.[39] In 1968, annual
debt service amounted to over $4 billion. At the beginning of that
year, 27.2 per cent of outstanding public and public-guaranteed
debts were owed to the United States, and 9.1 per cent to the

Soviet Union and the other Communist states in Eastern Europe. It is clear that this burden is becoming "oppressive" in the sense of operating strongly against further economic growth in the less developed states unless the volume of new aid increases markedly, which it shows no present signs of doing. When reaching critical proportions, debts are often renegotiated. Argentina's public debt was renegotiated three times in a decade, Indonesia's three times in three consecutive years. To the extent that renegotiation leads to relief, the grant element in loans is increased retroactively. Yet so far renegotiations have taken too little account of the fact that unmanageable debts are often not only the debtor's but also the creditor's fault. Both may have been too greedy and too careless. It is also apparent that the grant element in loans generally has been set too low, except perhaps in loans given by Communist states. The Pearson Committee recommended that "the terms of official development assistance loans should henceforth provide for interest of no more than 2 per cent, a maturity of between twenty-five and forty years, and a grace period of from seven to ten years."[40]

Of course, the grant element in aid can be reduced not only by financial conditions, shipping restrictions, etc., but also by non-economic conditions. A telling example of this has often occurred in the case of arms aid and military assistance. Some arms-exporting countries have stipulated in advance that their arms are to be used only in certain contingencies. Sometimes, the grant element is reduced retroactively and arbitrarily. The recipient of substantial military aid becomes dependent on the donor for replacements, spare parts, and ammunition, and thereby becomes vulnerable to pressure. When the United States and Britain laid on an arms embargo against India and Pakistan in 1965, their purpose was to bring the fighting between the two states to a halt. This may have been a noble purpose from their standpoint. But from the viewpoint of the Indian and Pakistani governments, this act constituted an infringement on their sovereignty, an essentially coercive act. This was even true, however worthy the cause seemed to the donor country, when the United States restricted resumed arms shipments to Pakistan once the latter was quelling the East Pakistan uprising in 1971.

There are other ways in which the recipient may pay for aid. One way may be through the "penetration" of the recipient country, which aid makes possible, and which may be used for the donor's purposes. We have noted in the foregoing how even the imposition of economic conditions on the proper use of aid, even the imposition of "virtue" suggests a semicolonial situation; and people in the recipient country may well resent the patronizing involved. In view of past colonial realities, they may be genuinely apprehensive of the dangers of neocolonialism. The flood of officials and technicians may well *look* to the suspicious mind like symbols of foreign domination and exploitation.

On the recipient side, too, the population cannot be regarded as a unitary actor. To *whom* do the benefits accrue, and *who* is saddled with the cost? Even if in some over-all sense the aggregate benefits exceed the aggregate costs (a calculation that cannot be made objectively, since subjective values are involved), some people, quite possibly a small minority, may get most of the benefits, and the others may bear most of the costs. All we can infer, when aid is received, is that the government authorities, and those with preponderant influence over them, regard the aid contract as a deal favorable in the *net*. Group and class conflict about the receipt of aid is therefore a common occurrence. Thus, if *A* gives economic or military aid to the government of *B*, it may well strengthen a regime that much of the population regards as reprehensible.

The fact that the acceptance of aid involves disutilities as well as utilities has elicited a number of reactions in the recipient countries. On the one hand, there are demands that economic aid should be more in amount and free of all the conditions that reduce its value. Especially in the younger generation of many less developed countries, there is the growing attitude that, as practiced, foreign aid is an insufficient down payment on account of injustices received in the colonial past.[41] On the other hand, some governments have preferred loans to grants in order to escape some of

the drawbacks, and occasionally recipient governments have themselves suspended aid. Many recipient governments have expressed
a preference for receiving aid through multilateral channels like the
specialized agencies and programs of the UN, because this vehicle
reduces the donor's viability of aid for his own purposes. Many
underdeveloped countries have also understood that rivalry between big donors is a condition which lowers the cost of receiving
aid and may, in addition, increase total aid receipts. The Cold
War rivalry between the two superpowers made "working both
sides of the street" a feasible tactic for a number of recipients
(e.g. India, Pakistan, Iran, Turkey). If aid is received from both
sides, the influence derivable by either is evidently diluted. However, the prospect of reaping these advantages depends on the
recipient country's being important to both big donors, each being
jealous of the influence achieved by the others, or by a third state,
and on the recipient's basic lack of political commitment, and
hence his disinterest in choosing sides. If he prefers one side but
must feign indifference in order to attract aid from both, he is
paying a price.[42]

   A third reaction of less developed countries has taken the form
of demanding improved access for their exports to the markets of
the highly developed states, instead of aid, or on top of aid. Thus,
at the United Nations Conference on Trade and Development
(UNCTAD), held in Geneva in 1964, the governments of these
states pressed for a general reduction of trade barriers for the
industrial exports of the developing countries. If this improved
access were based on preferences not extended to the exports of
all countries, the result would be a direct transfer of resources
from consumers in the developed countries to the industrializing
less developed states. Another demand was for higher prices for
raw-material exports of the less developed areas arranged by
means of international commodity agreements which would stabilize and raise prices through agreed export quotas or negotiated
prices. This practice again would transfer resources from consumers
in the importing countries to the less developed states. In either
case, such economic aid transferred by way of trade is exploitable

by the donor state only if the preferences are granted on a bilateral concessionary basis subject to renegotiation. This possibility would be greatly minimized were all highly developed states to extend identical preferences to all less developed states.

The *noneconomic* costs to the recipients vary but are clearly considerable, and their evaluation, unlike that of the economic ingredients, is complicated by its essentially subjective character. This is a subjectivity which does not reduce the reality of the evaluation process and outcome, and which is only in part capable of correction on objective grounds. All these noneconomic disadvantages are variables, to be sure, depressing the gross utility of receiving aid more in some cases than in others.

The conclusion of this analysis is not, of course, that foreign aid is a hoax or, worse, nothing but a neocolonial instrument by means of which the wealthy countries manipulate the poor. But neither is foreign aid the great and unmitigated boon to the less developed parts of the world, in which terms it is often described.

Notes

1. Cf. Jacob Viner, *International Economics,* pp. 347–348.
2. Barnett, *Communist China and America,* pp. 244–245.
3. *The New York Times* (Jan. 10, 1971; Feb. 10, 1971), p. 9; (March 14, 1971), p. 13.
4. *The New York Times* (December 28, 1971), p. 5.
5. "Sikkim Parties Share Hostility to China," *Hindustan Times* (June 1, 1967), p. 9.
6. *The New York Times* (March 5, 1971), p. 7.
7. Among the many discussions of foreign-aid motivations, see Goldman, *Soviet Aid,* pp. 185–192; Samuel P. Huntington, "Foreign Aid, For What, and For Whom," *Foreign Policy,* I (1971), pp. 125–126, 166–170; Erhard Eppler, "Entwicklungspolitik und Eigeninteressen," *Europa-Archiv,* 26 (25 Mar., 1971): 187–194.
8. Jacob J. Kaplan, *The Challenge of Foreign Aid* (New York: Praeger, 1967), p. 184.
9. Gilbert Comte, "Chad—the French are Here to Stay," *Le Monde* (Paris: Weekly Ed., May 13, 1970), p. 4.
10. *Ibid.*

11. Wu, *Economic Warfare*, p. 187.

12. Perroux, *L'economie du XXeme siècle*, pp. 324–325.

13. *Partners in Development*, Report of the Commission on International Development (New York: Praeger, 1969), p. 6.

14. Kindleberger, *Power and Money*, p. 142.

15. Albert O. Hirschman and Richard M. Bird, *Foreign Aid—A Critique and a Proposal* (Princeton: Princeton University Press, International Finance Section, Essays in International Finance, No. 69 (July, 1968), pp. 7–13).

16. Kaplan, *The Challenge of Foreign Aid*, pp. 215–216.

17. *The New York Times* (May 27, 1971), p. 9.

18. Charles Wolf, Jr., *Foreign Aid, Theory and Practice in Southern Asia* (Princeton: Princeton University Press, 1960), p. 38.

19. Wiles, *Communist International Economics*, p. 404.

20. *USSR and Third World*, A Survey of Soviet and Chinese Relations with Africa, Asia and Latin America, I, No. 3 (London: 1971), p. 98.

21. *Communist States and Developing Countries: Aid and Trade in 1969* (Washington: Department of State, Bureau of Intelligence and Research, July 9, 1970).

22. Cf. Uri Ra'anan, *The USSR Arms in the Third World, Case Studies in Soviet Foreign Policy* (Cambridge, Mass.: M.I.T. Press, 1969), pp. 159–161.

23. A. S. Becker and A. L. Horelick, *Soviet Policy in the Middle East*, (Santa Monica: The RAND Corp., 1970), pp. 29–30.

24. See *ibid.*, Part II; Uri Ra'anan, *The USSR Arms in the Third World*, pp. 168–172.

25. "National Diplomacy, 1965–1970," *Congressional Quarterly*, p. 24.

26. Eckstein, *Communist China's Economic Growth and Foreign Trade*, chap. V.

27. *Ibid.*, pp. 144–169.

28. *The New York Times* (March 23, 1971), p. 3.

29. *Ibid.*

30. See Stephen P. Gilbert, "Soviet-American Military Aid Competition in the Third World," *Orbis*, Vol. XIII (1970), pp. 1117–1137.

31. Kaplan, *The Challenge of Foreign Aid*, p. 144.

32. *Ibid.*, pp. 226–228.

33. Cf. Wu, *Economic Warfare*, p. 186.

34. Wolf, *Economic Aid*, p. 392.

35. Uri Ra'anan, *The USSR Arms in the Third World*, pp. 159–167.

36. One author has suggested that resource costs on Soviet aid programs have been only about 15 per cent of the aid formally extended. Calculating formal Soviet aid programs at $6296 million from 1955 to 1968, he maintains that only $3101 million were actually drawn upon. He then subtracts $1649 million as the value of expected repayments, and $711 million as aid-connected gains of trade, and thus arrives at an incredible $681 million! Cf. James Richard Carter, *The Net Costs of Soviet Foreign Aid* (New York: Praeger, 1969), Ch. 7.

37. Maxwell, *India's China War* (London: Jonathan Cape, 1970), pp. 270–271.

38. Kindleberger, *Power and Money*, p. 140.

39. *Partners in Development*, Ch. 8.

40. *Ibid.*, p. 164.

41. Eppler, "Entwicklungspolitik und Eigeninteressen," *Europa-Archiv* (Mar. 25, 1971), p. 192.

. 42. There are more complex situations inviting more complicated maneuvering by the recipient. See Albert O. Hirschman, "The Stability of Neutralism: A Geometric Note," in Bruce M. Russett (ed.), *Economic Theories of International Politics* (Chicago: Markham, 1968), Ch. 17.

CHAPTER

8

Summary and Conclusion

The principal points of the preceding analysis remain to be summarized. We will first present conclusions fitting both international military and economic power, and then turn to points peculiar to each form of national power.

Regarding National Military and Economic Power

1. A state's size (population and area) and wealth (GNP) do not yield military or economic power automatically. To achieve putative power ready for use, capabilities must be marshaled or mobilized for the express purpose of wielding power, and must be paid for in terms of opportunity costs. These costs turn on political and moral as well as economic values.

2. Putative power depends also on the skill of the mobilization effort, since skill controls the amount of suitable strength to be derived from resources allocated for the purpose.

3. The international use of putative power can serve several distinct functions. Most important are those of coercion and of the

forcible preservation or change of an international *status quo* without co-operation by a coerced actor. These are the main adversary uses of power, occurring in situations of conflict. Power can also be employed supportively to strengthen a weaker state economically or militarily, even though such support may be part of an adversary power play against a third state.

4. Between two states, the actualization of putative power through conflict is subject to several variable conditions, in addition to differences in putative strength, especially the comparative net values at stake, comparative domestic and foreign support, and relative rationality in the making and implementation of decisions. Among the factors which degrade rationality, especially in modern industrial states, lack of integration in the relevant activities of various parts of government and bureaucracy tends to be particularly important. These independent variables (and others usually of lesser weight or uncertain presence) combine differently in the particular situations in which power becomes more or less effective.

5. The actual effects of military and economic power plays depend, of course, on the precise circumstances of each peculiar case. To discern and weigh these peculiarities, and to predict their impact in a complex process of interaction, is usually difficult and leaves appreciable uncertainties.

6. National power works best when unchallenged, that is, when weaker actors dismiss or do not even consider courses of action which would risk conflict with stronger actors. Power becomes then effective without costs to the power holder. But the effectiveness of this "silent mechanism," through which power becomes effective without being wielded, depends upon expectations regarding the probability of a threat, if the interests of the stronger actor are crossed, and on the further probability of the threats being executed in the event the threat is defied.

7. National power works next best when a slight inferential threat—perhaps some ambiguous symbolic gesture or an informal cautionary remark in private discussion—made when conflict has

not acquired salience, suffices to affect the behavior of the weaker party. In that event, the costs of exerting power and of encountering it are small. But so are the issues at stake for both sides.

8. When power is employed supportively, effectiveness depends on the extent to which external support can make up for deficiencies in local strength or wealth. When such employment is ultimately directed against a third state, the latter's countermeasures also affect effectiveness.

9. Attempts at wielding national power are liable to fail when the target state can evade pressure by seeking relief from other states, and particularly from a state engaged in active and effective rivalry with the power-wielding country. Power tends to be greatest when it is monopolist. The normal availability of alternatives minimizes and frustrates monopolist power exercised for making economic threats more than for making military threats.

10. Since the international application of power is productive only if it secures values net of costs, longer-run costs must be balanced against any short-term payoffs; and these costs are hard to predict.

11. The fact that power confers options to be exercised in unknown future contingencies tends to make its cultivation attractive. But once power has been accumulated, the temptation to employ it seems hard to resist. If power corrupts, it does so in part by unprincipled yielding to this temptation.

12. Since the utility of both military and economic power has been diminishing in the contemporary world, the substitution of one for the other, though effective in cases of a particularly suitable structure of vulnerabilities or opportunities, does not generally offer appreciable possibilities. The trend in recent decades has been to lower the international utility of all adversary uses of power, especially when applied in salient conflict.

13. The present limitations besetting the actualization of military and economic national power would seem to make the cultivation of noncoercive forms of international influence more attractive and, with this, perhaps also call attention to a modi-

fication of the international system itself, so that its membership is spared the collective costs of national power plays, that is to say, the costs incurred by the wielder of power, target states, and third countries.

Regarding Military Power

1. The application of nuclear technology has made resort to military power, except for purposes of deterring a direct attack, more dangerous to major military powers and hence less usable and useful than was the case prior to World War II.

2. Another contemporary condition which tends to reduce the usability of military force is the normative devaluation of war as a legitimate instrument of policy except in self-defense.

3. Other conditions which have recently tended to diminish the utility of military power are (a) the rising state resistance to threats, and the increased difficulty of occupying and holding foreign territory, resulting from the spread of nationalism and the increasingly effective political organization of the economically less developed parts of the world; and (b) the decreased attractiveness of some objectives on behalf of which military force has often been used in the past, particularly gains in economic wealth and in certain bases of military strength (e.g. territory).

Regarding Economic Power

1. Unlike the use of military power, which small powers can initiate against other small states, the pursuit and exercise of national economic power is normally only for big and wealthy states (excepting occasionally small ones which are in possession of monopolist power over an indispensable source of supply).

2. When acting rationally, big and wealthy countries will subordinate the usual economic aims of economic policy to economic power plays only if they want international power badly enough, and crave it for other purposes as well as economic gain, or for noneconomic gains exclusively.

3. The vulnerability of countries to economic power plays is inherent in international economic interdependence which, though mutual, gives a substantial asymmetrical advantage to one side over the other.

4. In the light of recent history, the value of threatening economic reprisals cannot be considered high. What has made the threat value low is the sharpened sensitivity of poor and weak states to any attempt at coercion. For this reason, the value of economic threats seems, at present at least, subject to secular depreciation.

5. The limitations on the utility of international economic power do not extend to the use of economic advantages for purposes of *quid-pro-quo* bargaining, even when economic advantage is exchanged for a noneconomic payoff. But straight international exchanges do not involve the use of economic power.

Conclusion

The analysis of international power presented in this small volume is limited to the major problems. Their discussion can be extended to more subtle problems and supported by more ample and detailed case material. Moreover, as indicated in the preface, the present volume did not afford space for an examination of various associated problems. Particularly important among these are the bases and uses of informal penetration of one society by another (e.g. by means of propaganda, foreign investment, etc.); the bases and uses of nonpower influence between states and nations; the systematic exploration of international interdependencies; and theories of imperialism and neo-colonialism which focus normatively on certain configurations to which such interdependencies give rise. All of these matters will be presented in a second and larger book on which the author is working at the present time. Nevertheless, the present volume is self-contained and copes with the most fundamental problems posed by its title.

INDEX